WINCHESTER'S THREE BATTLES

A Civil War Driving Tour Through Virginia's Most War-Torn Town

Brandon H. Beck

By Brandon H. Beck

Angle Valley Press
WINCHESTER, VIRGINIA

For information contact:
Angle Valley Press, P. O. Box 4098, Winchester, VA 22604
www.AngleValleyPress.com

Designed and printed in the United States of America.

First Edition, First Printing

Cover Design—Radford Wine - www.radfordwine.com

Editor—John J. Fox III

Interior Design—1106 Design - www.1106design.com

Publisher's Cataloging-in-Publication Data
provided by Five Rainbows Cataloging Services

Names: Beck, Brandon H., 1944–
Title: Winchester's three battles : a driving tour through Virginia's most war-torn town / Brandon H. Beck.
Description: Winchester, VA : Angle Valley Press, 2016. | Includes bibliographical references.
Identifiers: LCCN 2016941992 | ISBN 978-0-9711950-6-6 (pbk.)
Subjects: LCSH: Winchester, 1st Battle of, Winchester, Va., 1862 (May 25) | Winchester, 2nd Battle of, Winchester, Va., 1863. | Winchester, 3rd Battle of, Winchester, Va., 1864. | Virginia--History--Civil War, 1861–1865--Campaigns. | Battlefields--Shenandoah River Valley (Va. and W. Va.)--Tours. | BISAC: HISTORY / United States / Civil War Period (1850–1877). | HISTORY / United States / State & Local / South (AL, AR, FL, GA, KY, LA, MS, NC, SC, TN, VA, WV). | HISTORY / Modern / 19th Century.
Classification: LCC E470.3 .B45 2016 (print) | LCC E470.3 (ebook) | DDC 975.5/041--dc23.

For Brian, Brian's family, and Kyle

CONTENTS

MAPS

ACKNOWLEDGMENTS

I AM INDEBTED TO THE FOLLOWING for helping make this book possible: Greig Aitken and Tonie Wallace of Historic Jordan Springs; Bill Austin, former Director of the Knowledge Point at Shenandoah University; Sandra Bosley, of Preservation of Historic Winchester, who prepared the manuscript; Patrick Fly, Frederick County [Va] IT & GIS, for the maps; John Fox of Angle Valley Press; Terry Heder, of the Shenandoah Valley Battlefields Foundation; Jonathan Noyalas my former student and now Director of the Center for Civil War Studies at Lord Fairfax Community College; Bob Price, for his photographs; Katherine Whitesell of the Fort Collier Civil War Center; and Radford Wine for the cover design.

We are all in debt to the Civil War Trust and to the Shenandoah Valley Battlefields Foundation for their preservation achievements in Winchester. They are changing the interpretive landscape. Guides and authors who have changed the historiographical landscape include Gary Ecelbarger, Jerry Holsworth, Larry Maier, Jonathan Noyalas and Scott Patchan. The Civil War Education Association, a fixture in the Civil War landscape under Bob Maher's direction, has long provided a public platform for authors and guides.

General Robert E. Lee (1807–1870)

As military advisor to President Davis and as commander of the Army of Northern Virginia, General Lee shared Stonewall Jackson's conviction that "if the Valley is lost, Virginia is lost." [Library of Congress]

INTRODUCTION

The Shenandoah Valley and Winchester

The Shenandoah Valley, the great Valley of Virginia, is an integral part of the Old Dominion, yet with an identity of its own. Lying between its western wall, the Alleghenies, and the Blue Ridge on the east, it stretches from Lexington down to the Potomac, about 140 miles to the northeast. One of Stonewall's veterans described the Valley's mountain walls as "monuments of God's greatness."

The small streams called the North Fork Shenandoah River and the South Fork Shenandoah River rise in the Upper (southern) Valley and finally come together as the Shenandoah River at Front Royal. It then flows north into the Potomac River at Harpers Ferry.

> Because the Forks of the Shenandoah River and the main stem Shenandoah River flow from south to north, military movement in the Valley from south to north is called "down" the Valley and movement from north to south is "up" the Valley. This is why the area around Winchester is known as the Lower Valley and the area southwest near Staunton is known as the Upper Valley. Failure to understand this will result in confusion.

The Valley is a place of great beauty and plenty. The first settlers to enter the Valley crossed the Potomac at Williamsport and headed south on what became known as the Great Wagon Road. By the mid-19th century, the Great Wagon

STONEWALL JACKSON

A

Character Sketch

"You may be what you resolve to be."
"Duty is ours, consequences are God's."
—Stonewall Jackson.

By
H. H. SMITH
Blackstone, Virginia.

PRICE 15 CENTS.
(Five or more copies 10 cents each).

Stonewall Jackson

Pamphlets such as this one, from 1910, combined contemporary and later accounts of Jackson's life. They were meant to memorialize his military virtues and draw lessons from his character. In Winchester, this was "preaching to the choir."

Road had become the macadamized Valley Pike, the predecessor to today's U.S. Route 11 and Interstate I-81.

The Valley is linked with the heart of the Old Dominion by road and rail. The Alleghenies to the west are an unforgiving range, more truly a mountain wall than the Blue Ridge. Gaps in the Blue Ridge are plentiful and easy to cross. In the Upper Valley of Staunton, the Virginia Central Railroad provided an excellent connection with the east. Valley farm produce could also be shipped east by road, rail, or water from nearby Lynchburg. In the Lower Valley, the Manassas Gap Railroad linked the Valley with the east from Mt. Jackson, by way of Strasburg, Front Royal, and Plains, and on to Manassas Junction. At Winchester, the frail Winchester & Potomac led to the mighty Baltimore & Ohio Railroad at Harpers Ferry.

The Valley was also rich in strategic options for the defense of Richmond, 150 miles east. A Confederate force coming down the Valley and crossing the Potomac was a spear hurled against the gates of the North, threatening Maryland, Pennsylvania, and even the District of Columbia. But by contrast the Valley deflected away from Richmond any Northern force coming south up the Valley. The Lower Valley became the strategic key to either a strategy of diversion, by pulling Union troops away from Richmond, or a strategy of invasion into the North. Due to its location, Winchester was the key to the Lower Valley.

Winchester's importance arose by default. In June 1861, Confederate general Joseph E. Johnston abandoned Harpers Ferry in favor of Winchester as the point from which to defend the Valley. The underlying geographical and military realities confirmed the wisdom of Johnston's decision.

Winchester is about 100 miles north of the railhead at Staunton, and only about 25 miles from the Manassas Gap Railroad at Plains (today's Delaplane). Its proximity to Manassas Junction was especially important in July 1861, when Johnston moved most of his command from Winchester to Manassas for the First Battle of Manassas (July 21). This historical first movement of troops by rail into battle led to the undying fame of one of Johnston's brigadiers, Thomas Jonathan "Stonewall" Jackson.

Winchester is also only 35 miles from the Potomac River crossings at Shepherdstown and Harpers Ferry, and only 40 miles from Williamsport. In the spring of 1862, Stonewall Jackson "threatened the line of the Potomac," after winning the First Battle of Winchester on May 25, 1862. In the summer of 1863, General Richard S. Ewell crossed the Potomac and moved to Carlisle and then Gettysburg, Pennsylvania, after winning the Second Battle of Winchester, on July 14–15, 1863. In the summer of 1864, General Jubal A. Early crossed the Potomac and marched toward Pennsylvania and then the District of Columbia. He recrossed the Potomac to the Valley, but remained a threat to the North until his defeat at the Third Battle of Winchester on September 19, 1864.

Winchester's wartime population was about 4,500, which included 788 free blacks and 655 slaves. It then and still is the county seat of Frederick County. The county's population was about 14,500 with 2,362 slaves.

It should be noted that in no Virginia county north or west of Frederick County was slavery as statistically or politically as important as it was here. It was in Winchester and the Lower Valley that many Union soldiers encountered the South's "peculiar institution" for the first time. One Union soldier noted what he described as "a lack of intelligence and enterprise throughout the region," which he attributed to the stultifying influence of slavery. He noted that it was a "sad sight to men who had been blessed with a home of intelligence and plenty in New England."

The number of roads converging at Winchester augmented its importance. In addition to the Valley Pike (known as the Martinsburg Pike north of Winchester), eight militarily important roadways converged at the hub of the Lower Valley. These were:

1. Old Charlestown Pike (today's Route 761), to Charlestown and Harpers Ferry
2. Berryville Pike (today's Route 7), east to Berryville, then over the Shenandoah River and the Blue Ridge at Snicker's Gap
3. Winchester (or Millwood) Pike (today's Route 50 East), to Upperville and points east, or to Delaplane and the closest connection with the Manassas Gap Railroad
4. Front Royal Pike (today's Route 522 South)
5. Middle Road (today's Route 628)
6. Cedar Creek Grade (today's Route 622), to Cedar Creek Gap through Little North Mountain
7. Northwest Turnpike (today's Route 50 West), to Romney, West Virginia

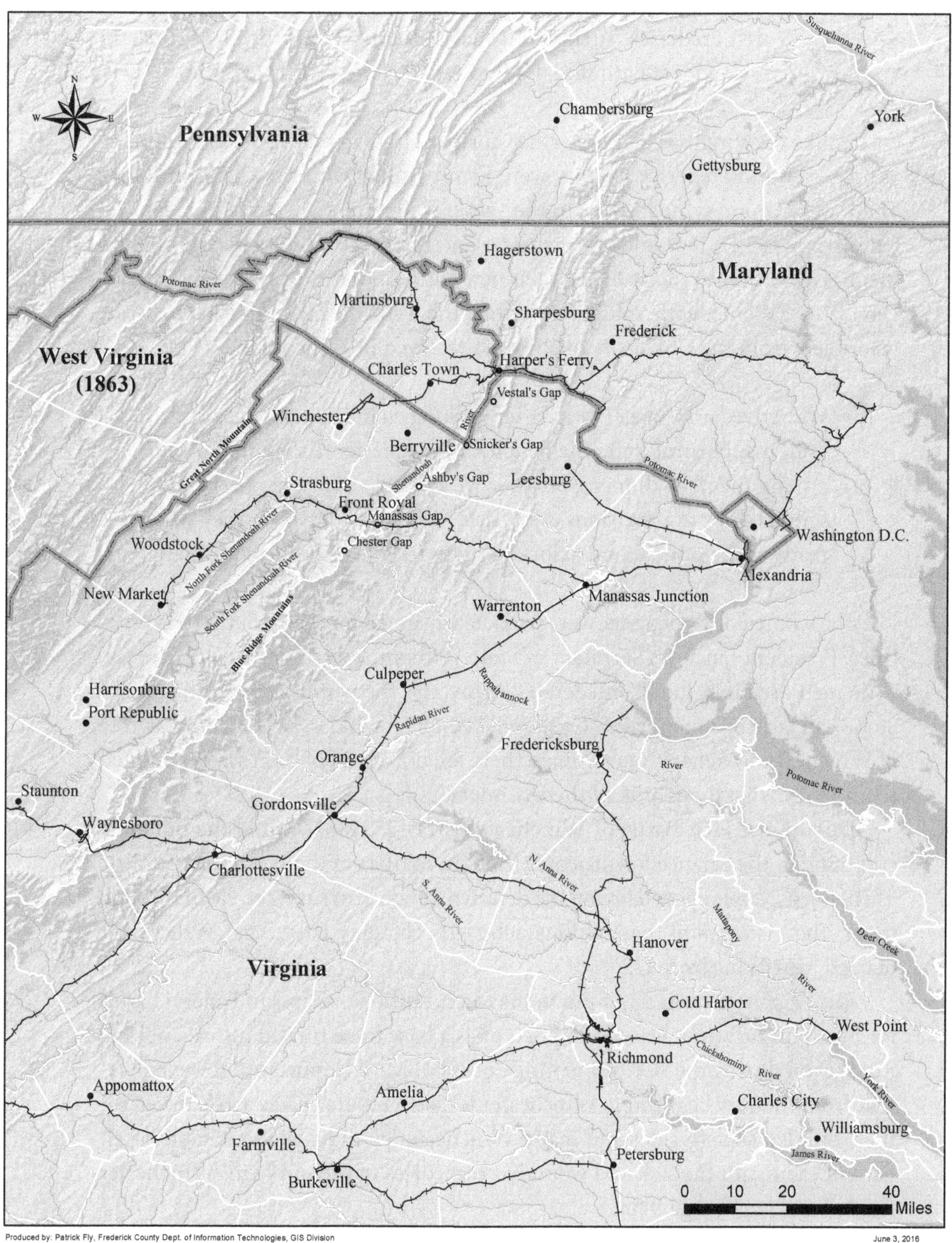

Produced by: Patrick Fly, Frederick County Dept. of Information Technologies, GIS Division

June 3, 2016

Virginia in the Eastern Theater of the War (1861–1865)
The Shenandoah Valley and Winchester

8. North Frederick Turnpike (today's Route 522 North), to Hancock, Maryland, via Bath (today's Berkeley Springs, West Virginia)

Unlike the Virginia counties farther north and west—today's West Virginia—Winchester and Frederick County were firmly linked with the Old Dominion. There were Union sympathizers in the Lower Valley, but when Virginia left the Union on April 17, 1861, most Winchester and Frederick County people aligned themselves with their old state and their new nation. Soon after secession, Charles Davidson, a Confederate soldier, described the welcome he and his compatriot volunteers from the University of Virginia received in Winchester.

> We arrived in Winchester . . . after walking eighteen miles over a hard road in a burning sun. The people of Winchester distributed us out among them for dinner, and after we arrived at Harpers Ferry they sent us a box of provisions every day . . . on our return . . . they were ready at the train at one o'clock at night to take us home with them.

The women of Winchester were particularly noted for their Southern sympathies. President Lincoln's Secretary of State William Seward said of Winchester, "The men are all in the [Confederate] Army and the women are all the devil." Stonewall Jackson's mapmaker, Captain Jedediah Hotchkiss, a New Yorker, wrote of Winchester's women: "Our women there are not afraid of the Yankees and tell them freely what they think of their conduct."

During the First Battle of Winchester (May 25, 1862), while the outcome still hung in the balance townspeople fired on soldiers of the 1st Maine Cavalry. Then, townspeople opened fire on the defeated Union army as it retreated through town. The historian of the 2nd Massachusetts Infantry wrote that Winchester needed "purifying by fire."

But Winchester was never put to the torch. Although it was in Federal hands for much of the war, it was too important as a base to be turned into a smoking mess, even during the "Great Burning" of 1864. Most important, however, was that from the very beginning, Winchester forged a reputation as a safe haven for the wounded of both sides and many Winchester civilians made notable sacrifices in caring for the sick and wounded regardless of the uniform. Winchester needed no "purifying by fire."

CHAPTER 1

THE BATTLES OF WINCHESTER: AN OVERVIEW

A great battle can never be regarded as a solitaire, a jewel to be admired or condemned for itself alone, without reference to surrounding objects and circumstances.

— General George B. McClellan

THE WAR CAME EARLY TO VIRGINIA. John Brown's Raid at Harpers Ferry in October 1859 reverberated throughout the Old Dominion. His execution in Charles Town (then in Virginia) in December 1859 loomed large in the Presidential election of 1860. The Virginia vote went to John Bell of the Constitutional Union Party. Bell won with just over 74,000 votes, defeating Southern Democrat John C. Breckenridge by 156 votes. Lincoln polled fewer than 2,000 votes. After the firing on Fort Sumter, however, Lincoln's call for troops led Virginia to secede on April 17, 1861.

The war came quickly to the Valley as well. Confederate troops in Winchester played an important role in the Battle of Manassas in July 1861. In November 1861, Stonewall Jackson was assigned to Winchester with a small force that included the Stonewall Brigade. That winter (1861–1862) he launched a campaign into today's West Virginia (the Romney Campaign) to forestall the probable Union invasion of the Lower Valley in the coming spring. On March 12, 1862, General Nathaniel P. Banks occupied Winchester. Jackson withdrew to the south. The war in the Valley now began in earnest and Winchester would become its most important battleground.

Despite its great importance, Winchester proved impossible to defend. Banks failed to hold the town in 1862 while General Robert H. Milroy repeated the failure in 1863. Then in the fall of 1864, General Jubal Early repeated this scenario for the Confederates. Between these battles the town swapped occupiers many times, 72 by local tradition. Winchester, like Gettysburg, was an important road center, but unlike Gettysburg, it lacked strong natural defenses. Winchester is open from the south and north, along the Valley Pike, today's Route 11. It is also open to the east, from the Berryville Pike, today's Route 7. To the west, a line of ridges dominates the town, providing good cover for flanking movement against its defenses.

First Battle of Winchester

May 25, 1862

General Thomas J. "Stonewall" Jackson's victory over General Nathaniel P. Banks seals the success of the Valley Campaign

Second Battle of Winchester

June 14–15, 1863

General Richard S. Ewell's victory over General Robert H. Milroy begins the Army of Northern Virginia's Pennsylvania Campaign

Third Battle of Winchester

September 19, 1864

General Philip Sheridan's victory over General Jubal Early ends Early's Valley Campaign.

The 33rd Virginia Battle Flag

Many Confederate regiments fought in all three of the battles at Winchester. Among the most illustrious were "Lee's Tigers," Louisiana regiments that fought here under three different commanders. The fabled Stonewall Brigade—the 2nd, 4th, 5th, 27th, and 33rd Virginia regiments also fought in all three Winchester battles. The battle flag of the 33rd Virginia is on display at Stonewall Jackson's Headquarters Museum in Winchester. [WFCHS Collection, Stewart Bell, Jr. Archives Room, Handley Regional Library, Winchester, VA]

CHAPTER 2

THE FIRST BATTLE OF WINCHESTER

MAY 25, 1862

General Military Situation

THE FIRST "ON TO RICHMOND" campaign ended for the Union with defeat on July 21, 1861, at Manassas (Bull Run). By late 1861, President Lincoln gave command of the Union army to General George B. McClellan. McClellan planned a bold and innovative campaign to take Richmond and, he thought, to end the War. He moved his huge force—it would grow to over 120,000 men—by troop transports down the Potomac River and into the Chesapeake Bay for a landing at Fort Monroe. Situated at the bottom of the Peninsula formed by the York and James rivers, Fort Monroe would be his first base for an advance of 80 miles to Richmond.

> Because the Forks of the Shenandoah River and the main stem Shenandoah River flow from south to north, military movement in the Valley from south to north is called "down" the Valley and movement from north to south is "up" the Valley. This is why the area around Winchester is known as the Lower Valley and the area southwest near Staunton is known as the Upper Valley. Failure to understand this will result in confusion.

President Lincoln was unsure of McClellan's plan, fearing that it might expose Washington to attack. He gave it only conditional approval, requiring McClellan to keep 30,000 men at Fredericksburg under General Irvin McDowell. Also, General Nathaniel Banks' force of about 12,000 would remain in the Valley.

At first, the plan seemed to work well. The move to the peninsula forced Confederate General Joseph E. Johnston to abandon northern Virginia and concentrate nearly all his men—about half of McClellan's eventual total—at the peninsula to oppose McClellan. But neither Johnston, President Davis, nor Davis' military advisor, Robert E. Lee could have known yet that McClellan would be wracked with doubt, convinced that he was outnumbered and badly in need of the Union troops in the Valley and at Fredericksburg.

> *My religious belief teaches me to feel as safe in battle as in bed. God has found the time for my death. I do not concern myself about that, but to be always ready, no matter when it may overtake me.*
>
> — General Thomas J. "Stonewall" Jackson

The largest Confederate force in the Valley was Jackson's command at Winchester, originally about 3,000 men. Jackson's force was small, but his personal history shows a man who could accomplish much with little more than determination. He was orphaned early, poorly educated, but drove himself to overcome all handicaps. He willed himself to succeed at West Point. He then served with distinction in the Mexican War. He resigned from the peace time army to accept a professorship at the Virginia Military Institute. There he willed himself to become a teacher as he had willed himself to become a student. It was in Lexington that he came to his Presbyterian faith. His biographer, James I. Robertson, Jr., has shown that his faith was the most important sustaining force in his character and life and paid by his determination.

In the spring of 1862, Jackson's orders from Richmond were clear: he was to keep Federal forces already in the Valley from leaving for Fredericksburg and then on to the peninsula. It was a formidable task.

Nothing daunted, Jackson told Henry Kyd Douglas, a staff officer:

> My plan is to put on as bold a front as possible and to use every means in my power to prevent his advance, whilst our reorganization is going on . . . What I desire is to hold the country as far as practicable until

> we are in a condition to advance, and then with God's blessing, let us make thorough work of it. But let us start right.

But in March 1862, it was the Federals, not Jackson, who would "start right." Jackson's force was not strong enough to prevent Banks from occupying Winchester on March 12. Then several days later, thinking that Jackson had left the Valley, Banks, with significant pressure from General McClellan, ordered most of his force to cross the Blue Ridge, bound for Manassas and Fredericksburg. When Jackson learned from his cavalry leader, Colonel Turner Ashby, that most of the Federals had departed Winchester leaving behind a small force, he decided to strike. However, Brigadier General James Shields' division had not departed Winchester yet. This Federal force was three times larger than what Jackson expected. The result was that Jackson was defeated at the First Battle of Kernstown on March 23, 1862. He then retreated to a defensive position at Rude's Hill just south of Mount Jackson.

Kernstown is just beyond Winchester's southern city limit on U.S. Route 11 South, the Old Valley Pike. One block west of the Valley Pike lies the historic Pritchard-Grim Farm, within the core area of the First and Second Battles of Kernstown. This 315-acre parcel has been preserved through the efforts of the Kernstown Battlefield Association and public grants from local, state, and federal agencies. The prominent feature of the farm is Pritchard's Hill, which was the Union artillery position in both battles and a frequent observation post during periods of Union occupation of Winchester. Also present is the 1854 Pritchard House, a three-story brick home built by the family of the first settlers on the property. The battlefield park is open to the public on weekends from May through October each year. A series of six outdoor interpretive markers describe the actions that occurred there. KBA volunteers staff a Visitor Center from the second Saturday in May to the last Sunday in October from 10 AM to 4 PM on Saturdays and 12 noon to 4 PM on Sundays. Other access may be arranged by appointment. Contact *kba@kernstownbattle.org* for details.

The Battle of Kernstown marked Winchester's first experience with the horrors of a Civil War battlefield. Wounded and dying men from both sides were brought to Winchester, filling homes and buildings. One eyewitness described the scene in front of the courthouse on Loudoun Street, where the Confederate monument now stands:

> In the courtyard were two pieces of artillery, twelve pounders, taken from the enemy. In the vestibule lay thirteen dead bodies of United States soldiers and the courtroom was filled to its capacity with wounded . . . A Confederate captain, Yancey Jones, was lying there with both eyes scooped out and the bridge of his nose carried away by a bullet. He was sometimes delirious and roared about forming his company and charging.

Another significant result of the First Battle of Kernstown was that Jackson's tactical defeat became a strategic victory due in large part to Union General James Shields stating that his Federal forces defeated a Confederate force at least twice his size. Jackson's fierce attack, while it was repulsed, still halted the march of Banks' troops across the Blue Ridge. Banks' men reversed course and returned to the Valley. This move created much discussion amongst Confederate authorities

Confederate Monument

The Confederate monument was unveiled in 1916 in front of the Frederick County Courthouse on Loudoun Street. In 1862, wounded soldiers filled the square in front of the court building. [WFCHS Collection, Stewart Bell, Jr. Archives Room, Handley Regional Library, Winchester, VA]

in Richmond. They wondered if a Confederate defeat in the Valley had those consequences, then what might a victory accomplish?

Jackson believed he knew the answer—and so did Robert E. Lee. Both came to believe that a successful diversionary campaign in the Valley would not only hold Union forces in the Valley, but would also draw additional thousands to the Valley.

In early May, to counter a Union threat to Staunton, Jackson moved up the Valley and then west, to McDowell. There he joined General Edward Johnson's force of 2,800 men, giving him close to 10,000 men. On May 8 he fought General Robert Milroy's smaller force at McDowell. The Federals retreated west the next day.

At this point, President Lincoln felt secure enough to order Shields' division to move to join Irvin McDowell's troops at Fredericksburg. The combined force—Shields and McDowell would then move southeast to the Peninsula and reinforce McClellan's attack against Richmond. Banks remained behind in the Valley with the brigade of colonels Dudley Donnelly and George Gordon, five companies of cavalry and 16 cannons—in all less than 10,000 men. He occupied a strong position at Strasburg, twenty miles south of Winchester. Banks placed about 1,000 troops under Colonel Robert Kenly at Front Royal, to guard the bridges over the forks of the Shenandoah River.

Meanwhile, in Richmond, General Lee persuaded General Johnston and President Davis that Jackson should be reinforced with General Richard S. Ewell's division, then south of Fredericksburg. Ewell soon received orders to move his division west into the Valley.

This reinforcement became the key to Jackson's plans because he knew that the time to strike had come. He concentrated his force—now about 17,000, counting Ewell—at New Market, on May 20. His men then marched through the New Market Gap into the Luray Valley and turned north toward Front Royal. He used the Massanutten Mountain range to screen his left flank. Jackson hoped to cross the Shenandoah River over the Front Royal bridges and possibly destroy Banks' force as it retreated down the Valley from Strasburg to Winchester.

In the Battle of Front Royal on May 23, Jackson routed Kenly's small force, capturing most of it. He then moved his men over the Shenandoah River bridges.

Banks did not depart Strasburg for Winchester until the morning of May 24, his column trailing a long wagon train. Jackson hoped to attack the column before it reached Winchester, but he did not want to fight at Kernstown again, and he was also wary of the high ground—Bowers Hill, on the southern edge of town, which overlooked the Valley Pike. He sent Ewell's division, less General Richard Taylor's Louisiana brigade, toward Winchester on the Front Royal Pike, today's Route 522. Jackson kept Taylor's brigade with his own division, which followed Banks toward Winchester on the Valley Pike, today's Route 11. The Confederates pursued and harassed Banks' men but were unable to disrupt the column's progress. Banks reached Winchester on May 24. The First Battle of Winchester flared up early the next morning along the Valley Pike (Valley Avenue) and the Front Royal Pike (Millwood Avenue).

Of the three battles of Winchester the First Battle has lost most of its battlefield property to commercial and residential development. For this reason I have divided the tour into two parts. The first part covers Strasburg and Front Royal, and then Jackson's pursuit of Banks to Winchester. It includes seldom visited and still pristine sites, but it can be omitted if time is short. It begins and ends at the Winchester-Frederick County Visitor's Center, where the second part of the tour, covering just the battle sites in Winchester also begins and ends.

First Battle of Winchester Tour 1A

Part I

DRIVING TIME APPROXIMATELY 2½ HOURS—Driving directions are sans serif and indented

Point of Departure—Winchester-Frederick County Visitor's Center

STOP 1 Banks' Fort in Strasburg

STOP 2 Buckton Station

STOP 3 Battle of Front Royal Commemorative Marker

STOP 4 The Warren County Courthouse

STOP 5 Asbury Chapel

STOP 6 Prospect Hill Cemetery

STOP 7 **South Fork Crossing Site**

STOP 8 **"Riverside"**

STOP 9 **Fairview, the McKay House**

STOP 10 **Wayside Inn**

POINT OF DEPARTURE:

Winchester-Frederick County Visitor;s Center

1400 S. Pleasant Valley Road

(Pleasant Valley Road and Millwood Avenue)

Open daily 9:00–5:00

The Winchester-Frederick County Civil War Orientation Center provides background for all local Civil War history. The telephone number is (540) 542-1326 or toll free (877) 871-1326

www.visitwinchesterva.com/civil-war-orientation-center

For Front Royal information, contact Warren (Front Royal) Heritage Society, 101 Chester Street, Front Royal, VA 22630. (540) 636-1446. Also, contact the Front Royal Visitors Center at 414 E. Main Street or call (800) 338-2576 or (540) 635-5788.

Part I—Background Note

By May 12, Jackson decided not to attack Banks in a fortified position, such as Banks' Fort in Strasburg because his goal was not to take Strasburg, but instead to descend on Front Royal via the Luray Valley. By crushing Colonel Kenly's force, in the Battle of Front Royal on May 23, he seized and crossed the bridges over the Forks of the Shenandoah. This put him in position to destroy Banks' force before it could retreat to Winchester. To disrupt communication between Banks and Kenly, he sent Colonel Ashby's cavalry to Buckton Station, on the railroad between Strasburg and Front Royal, to cut the telegraph and destroy the railroad bridge over Passage Creek.

This trip features incredibly beautiful Shenandoah Valley scenery "where the Blue Ridge meets the Shenandoah" as well as seldom visited, almost unknown Civil War sites.

STOP 1 BANKS' FORT IN STRASBURG

To reach Stop 1, Banks' Fort in Strasburg, depart the Visitors Center and turn left onto Pleasant Valley Road. Turn left at the first stoplight which is Millwood Avenue. Go to the second light and turn left following the signs to I-81 south. Enter I-81 south go about 15 miles to exit 298 [Strasburg/Rt. 11]. As you approach Stephens City (old Newtown), note the Massanutten Range looming in the near distance. Pass the exits for Stephens City and Middletown. Take Exit 298 and turn left onto Rt. 11. After 1.1 miles the road crosses Hupps Hill, where a visit to the new Hupps Hill Civil War Park is highly recommended. The water tower visible ahead marks the site of Banks' Fort. As you enter town turn right on Rt 55 west. Go several streets and turn left on Banks Fort Road and drive uphill. There is room to park next to the water tower. Get out, and take in the views across the Valley.

Hupps Hill Civil War Park
33229 Old Valley Pike
Strasburg, VA
(540) 465-5884

STOP 2 BUCKTON STATION

To reach Stop 2, Buckton Station, turn left on Banks Fort Road and then turn left on North Street. Turn right on Route 11 and pass under the tracks of the

Old Manassas Gap Railroad. Turn left at the first light on Route 55 and cross the railroad tracks. You are now on the Old Strasburg Road. The old Manassas Gap RR station, now a museum, is ahead on the right. Massanutten Mountain is now directly ahead, as the road, railroad, and North Fork of the Shenandoah River run roughly parallel towards Front Royal. You will drive about 6 miles. Once you cross over Passage Creek, take the 2nd left onto Rt. 614. Bear left at fork onto Rt. 610. Cross railroad tracks and stop here as location is Buckton Station, Stop 2.

(**NOTE:** Be extremely careful here as trains ***DO*** run on this line!)

The Union defended this position from along the embankment. Ashby's cavalry charged from the fields to your left. Edwin E. Bryant, adjutant of the 3rd Wisconsin infantry, and Edwin L. Hubbard, company commander, stationed here on May 23, 1862, recalled the skirmish. According to Bryant:

> In front of the railroad on the southern side was a wheatfield and back of it a large wood. In this timber out of sight of Hubbard's pickets Ashby's cavalry—about 400—massed. At 2 o'clock they charged across the wheatfield, with a whoop and yell, two or three officers in front swinging their sabers . . . Three gallant Confederate cavalry charges and three desperate Federal volleys followed.

Captain Hubbard claimed that neither his company, nor "the brave Indianans flinched" in the face of Ashby's first charge. The Hoosiers fired one volley, and then a second from behind the railroad. "Horses fell," Hubbard said of this second volley, "others, riderless, ran in two directions; two or three of the cavalry charged up to the fill or embankment, but were killed before they got back. Among them was Captain Fletcher, a splendidly mounted and fine-looking officer. His followers broke and fell back into the timber in confusion and at a breakneck pace."

Ashby was able to burn the station and cut the wire, but could not take the bridge.

STOP 3 BATTLE OF FRONT ROYAL COMMEMORATIVE MARKER

To reach Stop 3, the Battle of Front Royal Commemorative Marker, turn around and carefully recross the tracks. Follow Rt 610 until it merges into Rt 626 which leads back to Route 55. At Rt 55 turn left and head east toward Front Royal. You will come to a light at Rt 340 and here it is also called North Shenandoah Avenue. Turn right and cross the North and South Forks of the Shenandoah River. As you near the light stay in left lane and turn left onto 14th Street. Continue and go straight through the intersection with North Commerce Avenue. The road becomes North Royal Avenue. Just beyond 4th Street turn left at the Y onto Chester Street. You will see Stop 3, the Battle of Front Royal Commemorative Monument, at the Y intersection of Royal and Chester. The monument was dedicated and unveiled on the sixty-first anniversary of the Battle of Front Royal, on May 23, 1927. A bronze tablet on the monument describes the battle as "the first move in Jackson's celebrated Valley Campaign."

Battle of Front Royal marker

At the corner of Royal and Chester in Front Royal. This monument was dedicated in 1927. [John Fox]

STOP 4 THE WARREN COUNTY COURTHOUSE

Continue straight on Chester Street and you will pass the Warren Rifles Confederate Museum on the left [95 Chester St.] This is worth a stop if you have time. Chester Street will dead end into E. Main Street where you will turn right. At the light you will intersect with North Royal Avenue. The Warren County Courthouse, Stop 4, is on your left.

The Confederate monument was dedicated on July 4, 1911 before a crowd of between six and seven thousand people. Mrs. Eleanor Richardson unveiled the monument. The inscription honors all Confederate veterans:

> "He hears the bugle calling over the vast mystic sea, for he tramped the fields with Stonewall, and climbed the heights with Lee."

Warren County Court House

The Confederate monument was dedicated in 1911 [John Fox]

STOP 5 ASBURY CHAPEL

Turn left onto North Royal Avenue and head south for about 4 miles. As you leave town the road will change to Rt 340 south. Jackson approached Front Royal from our next stop, Asbury Chapel. Look for the chapel on the right as it can be easy to miss. Pull into the chapel parking lot and get out to examine the historical marker here. This Virginia Civil War Trails marker describes how Jackson left the main road here, to make his advance as an indirect, concealed route.

Samuel Simpson of the 7th Virginia guided Jackson to today's Rocky Lane, which is only 400 feet farther on the highway.

Asbury Chapel today

[John Fox]

Asbury Chapel image from 19th century
[Virginia Civil War Trails]

Exit the chapel and turn right onto Rt 340 south but exercise caution as you will make an almost immediate left turn onto Rocky Lane [Rt 607]. This lane was known then as Gooney Manor Road or Snake Road. It was little more than a farm lane. Follow it uphill to where Jackson turned left onto the Browntown Road (Rt 649).

Drive several miles and you will see Church of Jesus Christ of Latter-Day Saints on the left. Pull into the parking lot and drive to the Civil War Trails marker near the road.

The marker describes the Rebel spy Belle Boyd's daring exploit to reach Jackson as he neared town. The 1st Maryland (CSA) led the Confederate advance into town, along with Major Roberdeau Wheat's battalion of Louisiana "Tigers." The heaviest fighting was between the 1st Maryland CSA and its Union counterpart, the 1st Maryland USA. Colonel Kenly attempted to cover his Marylanders with artillery fire from Camp Hill, close to his headquarters, while Jackson moved his guns to Academy Hill, near Prospect Hill, which is our next stop.

STOP 6 PROSPECT HILL CEMETERY

Turn left out of the church parking lot onto Browntown Road/Rt 649. Drive downhill to intersection with Rt 340. Turn right and drive back into Front Royal on Royal Avenue. Turn left on Prospect Street and drive to the cemetery entrance. Continue on to the summit to reach the Soldiers' Circle and park.

The Soldiers' Circle is the burial ground for 275 Confederate soldiers, including 185 unknown soldiers. The monument was unveiled in 1882. The dead include some of those killed in the Battle of Front Royal, but most of these soldiers died of sickness or wounds in Front Royal hospitals throughout the war. Front Royal celebrates its Confederate Memorial Day here every May 23rd. A short distance downhill is the Mosby Monument, dedicated in 1899. It memorializes seven of Mosby's Rangers (officially the 43rd Battalion of Virginia Cavalry) captured and executed by the Federals in Front Royal on September 23, 1864. Stonewall Jackson may have viewed the Battle of Front Royal from this location, but this was not a Confederate artillery position. Confederate guns were on the nearby Academy Hill.

Prospect Hill Cemetery
[John Fox]

STOP 7 SOUTH FORK CROSSING SITE

To reach Stop 7, the South Fork Crossing site, depart the cemetery back to Royal Avenue. Turn left onto North Royal Avenue. As you pass 13th Street near top of hill bear right at the 90 degree turn in road. You will still be on North Royal Avenue. After several blocks go under the railroad overpass. Pass by the V.F.W. Post #1860 on your right. The road ends just ahead; the Civil War Trails marker here describes the all-important crossing site for both forks of the Shenandoah River.

On your right note the railroad bridge. Taylor's 8th Louisiana Regiment crossed the smoldering bridge. Richard Taylor remembered:

> The 8th Regiment was on the right of my line, near at hand; and dismounting, Colonel Kelly led it across under a sharp musketry

> fire. Several men fell to disappear in the dark water beneath; but the movement continued with great rapidity, considering the difficulty of walking on timbers, and Kelly with his leading files gained the opposite shore. As the 8th Louisiana completed its crossing and flanked Kenly on his left, Flournoy's cavalry could be seen approaching Kenly's right. Having successfully isolated Kenly from Strasburg by disrupting communication along the railroad, they were now attempting his rear.

"At half-past 4 o'clock," according to Charles Camper of the First Maryland Regiment (Union), "the Colonel received information that a regiment of cavalry was in his rear, beyond the river, and rapidly advancing." Kenly checked and found that Colonel Thomas Flournoy's 6th Virginia cavalry threatened the Union supply depot at Riverton, in his rear. Colonel Kenly then ordered his men across the North Fork and they torched the bridge.

However, none of the bridges would burn. Gary Ecelbarger, author and battlefield guide, has pointed out that the spring of 1862 was the wettest the Shenandoah Valley would see until 1902, and that the bridges' new green wood would only smolder, and not burst into flame.

South Fork Shenandoah River Crossing Site

[John Fox]

STOP 8 "RIVERSIDE"

Retrace your route to W. 17th Street. Turn right there and then turn right onto N. Shenandoah Avenue [Rt340/522 north]. Cross South Fork Shenandoah River and make next right turn at light. This is E. Strasburg Road. Make next right onto Old Winchester Pike. "Riverside" is the large brick house directly south of the church. Jackson is said to have spent the night of May 23 here and to have written a note of thanks to Belle Boyd here.

STOP 9 THE MCKAY HOUSE, FAIRVIEW

Return to North Shenandoah Avenue [Rt 340/522 north]. Turn right. Drive 3.2 miles and just over rise see large house on right and pull into parking lot for Fairview.

Colonel Kenly made his "last stand" on the open plateau here. This is the site of one of the great cavalry charges of the war when the 2nd and 6th Virginia Cavalry regiments shattered Kenly's Union line of battle. Kenly fell wounded. His casualties totaled 773 with 691 men taken prisoner, most of them at Fairview. The Confederate loss was 36 killed and wounded. Among the Confederate prizes was the regimental flag of the 1st Maryland (Union). Soldiers entrusted it to Miss Nannie McKay of the house. She kept it until 1880 and then presented it to Maryland native and Confederate general Bradley Johnson at the unveiling of the Maryland Monument in the Stonewall Cemetery in Winchester.

The house today is silent, almost derelict. Its bloodstained floors speak for the wounded cared for here.

After resting his men on the night of May 23, Jackson hoped to break up Banks' command as it retreated north down the Valley. He did not want to give Banks time to make a stand at Kernstown, or on Bowers Hill just south of Winchester.

Jackson sent Ewell's troops ahead on the Front Royal Pike (Route 522 North). He took his division, along with General Richard Taylor's brigade from Ewell's division west to the Valley Pike (Route 11 North) via the former Old Chapel Road, now called Reliance Road.

> To follow Jackson's route, turn right on Rt 522 North. Go 100 yards to the first median crossover and do a U-turn heading back south. Go past Blue Ridge Shadows Golf Course on the right. At the light turn right onto Reliance Road [Rt 627]. It leads to Middletown about 6.5 miles ahead on the Valley Pike.

Jackson did not succeed in breaking up Banks' command for several reasons. Had he done so there would not have been a Battle of Winchester the next day. His advance on Reliance Road was painfully slow, in contrast to Banks' rapid retreat down the Valley Pike from Strasburg. Jackson's route was narrow, winding, and heavily wooded. Rain and mud slowed the pace even more.

Union colonel Calvin Douty, with 400 troopers conducted a skillful and stubborn retreat ahead of Jackson's Confederates on Reliance Road. Douty's men bought time for Banks to clear Middletown before Jackson could arrive. Then when Jackson did reach Middletown he initially turned south, thinking Banks could not have come this far. Douty's men paid a heavy price in the streets of Middletown for their rear guard action, but this resistance enabled Banks to put more distance between his own retreat and Jackson's pursuit.

Meanwhile, Ewell reached the old Double Tollgate on the Front Royal Pike [Rt 522]. He halted there waiting for instructions which never came. Several hours later his men moved on to camp just outside Winchester near the junction of the Front Royal and Millwood Pikes.

McKay House today, Fairview

[John Fox]

McKay House, Fairview war era

[Virginia Civil War Trails]

STOP 10 WAYSIDE INN

When you reach Middletown, at Route 11, turn left for a very short distance and note the Wayside Inn, Stop 10, on the right. The marker in front of the Inn describes Jackson's pursuit from here to Stephens City, Bartonsville and Winchester.

There were rear guard actions all the way, and two larger clashes at Stephens City. But Jackson would not slacken his pace nor rest his men until they had moved north of Kernstown. Only then did he allow a brief halt.

Turn around and drive north on Rt 11. Turn right on Reliance Road/Rt 627. Just before you reach I-81 there is a historical marker on the left for Jackson's Camp. Confederate legend has it that Jackson and Col. Turner Ashby kept watch while men slept all around them. Follow the signs for I-81 North, just ahead. Go North on I-81 and take Exit 313 for Winchester and the Visitors Center, following signs for Route 50 West. Stay in right lane and go to third traffic light and turn right on Millwood Avenue. Turn right onto Pleasant Valley Road. The Visitors Center is directly on the right.

Wayside Inn today

[John Fox]

First Battle of Winchester Tour 1B

To understand and follow the battle, keep three important landmarks in mind. First is Abram's [Abraham's] Creek. It runs along the southern edge of town from west to east. Second is Camp Hill, on Millwood Avenue, between Abram's Creek and the center of town. Camp Hill was Ewell's objective. Third is the high ground on the southwestern edge of town, Bowers Hill, just north of Abram's Creek. Bowers Hill was Jackson's main objective.

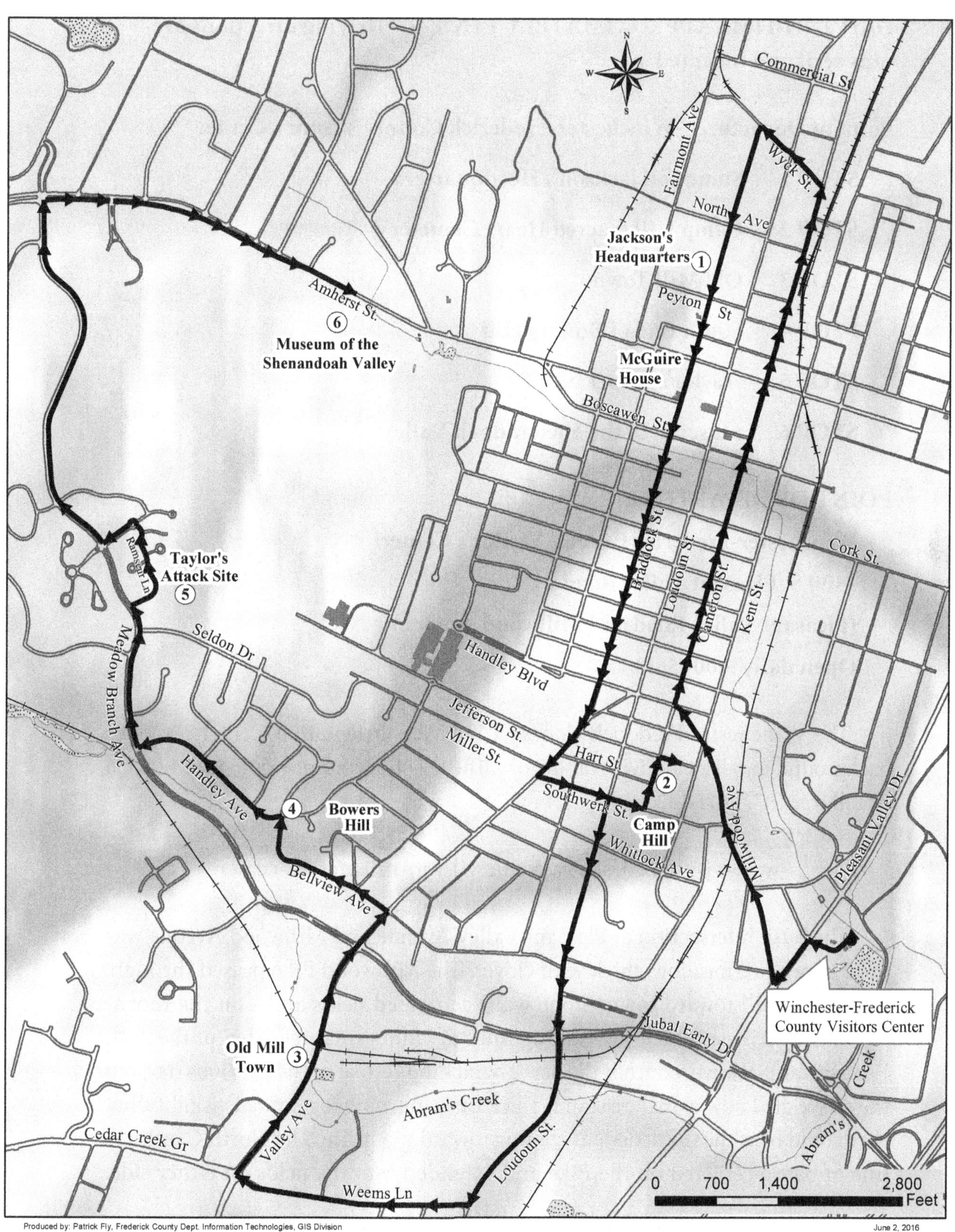

First Battle of Winchester, May 25, 1862
Tour 1B

DRIVING TIME APPROXIMATELY 1 HOUR—Driving directions are sans serif and indented

Point of Departure—Winchester-Frederick County Visitor's Center

STOP 1 Stonewall Jackson's Headquarters

STOP 2 Camp Hill (Sacred Heart Cemetery)

STOP 3 Old Mill Town

STOP 4 South End of Bowers Hill

STOP 5 Taylor's Attack Site

STOP 6 Museum of the Shenandoah Valley

POINT OF DEPARTURE:

Winchester-Frederick County Visitor's Center

1400 S. Pleasant Valley Road

(Pleasant Valley Road and Millwood Avenue)

Open daily 9:00–5:00

The Winchester-Frederick County Civil War Orientation Center provides background for all local Civil War history. The telephone number is (540) 542-1326 or toll free (877) 871-1326

www.visitwinchesterva.com/civil-war-orientation-center

The busy intersection of Pleasant Valley Avenue and Millwood Avenue was once a tranquil meadow, thick with clover. The Millwood Pike passed through, heading uphill toward town. Stone walls separated fields and—on the morning of May 25—sheltered the waiting lines of Union infantry. Men of the 46th Pennsylvania were tired from the nerve-wracking retreat of the previous day, but they were glad now to make a stand. Thick early morning fog limited visibility, but they could hear the Confederates coming toward them. The 21st North Carolina's line of battle centered on the Pike and extended into the fields on either side.

The North Carolinians never saw the Yankees until too late—if they saw them at all. They must have heard the Yankees rise to their feet, accoutrements rattling as the Pennsylvanians leveled their rifles and fired a tremendous volley into the Tar Heel ranks. The 21st North Carolina's colonel fell, badly wounded. Sixty-five of his men were killed or wounded. The volley halted Ewell's advance and it seemed clear that Banks planned to make a stand. However, the battle would not be decided here on the Millwood Pike, instead, the outcome lay in Jackson's hands, on the Valley Pike several miles to the west.

STOP 1 STONEWALL JACKSON'S HEADQUARTERS

Jackson's Headquarters

A view of the present day entrance to the Jackson's Headquarters site on Braddock Street. The house front faces to the left in this picture. The house is owned and maintained by the Winchester-Frederick County Historical Society. There are guided tours, museum displays, and a gift and bookstore inside. (540) 667-3242. Open April 1–October 31, Monday through Saturday 10 AM–4 PM, Sunday 12 noon–4 PM. Admission is $5. [Bob Price]

To reach our first stop, Jackson's Headquarters Museum, leave the Visitors Center. Turn left and then at the intersection turn right and head uphill on Millwood Avenue toward town. Cross the railroad tracks, proceed to the 2nd traffic light and turn right onto South Cameron Street, heading north. Proceed through the 3rd traffic light (Piccadilly Street). Continue straight for five blocks. (The railroad tracks on your right mark the line of the Civil War era Winchester & Potomac Railroad.) Turn left onto Wyck Street. Go through one traffic light, and then take the next left onto Braddock Street. At the end of the second block, look for the signs and markers on the right for Stonewall Jackson's Headquarters, at 415 N. Braddock St.

The house served as General Thomas J. "Stonewall" Jackson's military headquarters from early November 1861 until March 11, 1862. The museum contains numerous artifacts that belonged to both General Jackson and General Turner Ashby, as well as uniforms, swords, muskets, etc. The house appeared in two scenes in the movie *Gods and Generals.*

After your visit, continue south on Braddock Street for 1.1 miles to our next stop but notice the following sites on the way.

On the right at 319 N. Braddock St. is the house of Presbyterian pastor James R. Graham. Jackson and his wife, Anna, stayed in the outbuilding in the back.

At 103-105 N. Braddock St., at the corner of Amherst Street is the red brick house of Dr. Hunter McGuire, Jackson's friend and doctor. McGuire later became medical director of the Army of Northern Virginia and founder of the Medical College of Virginia.

The McGuire House

The McGuire House at Braddock and Amherst Streets was the home of Dr. Hunter McGuire, Stonewall Jackson's physician and later medical director of the Army of Northern Virginia. According to Winchester historian Ben Ritter, Jackson dined here one day in October or November 1862 before sitting for a portrait in Nicholas Routzahn's nearby studio. Mrs. Jackson called that image, the "crooked button" picture, her husband's best likeness. [Bob Price]

Stonewall Jackson, the "Crooked Button" Picture

The famous picture was taken in the fall of 1862. Ben Ritter has cited the Reverend Graham, who was present when the picture was taken: "When the general faced the camera, it was noticed that a button was missing from his coat . . . He answered at once, 'It's in my pocket. If you have a needle, I will sew it on . . .' " It's the third from the top on the left breast. [Charles Affleck Collection, Stewart Bell, Jr. Archives Room, Handley Regional Library, Winchester, VA]

STOP 2 CAMP HILL (SACRED HEART CEMETERY)

To reach Stop 2, the Sacred Heart Cemetery, continue on Braddock Street from Stonewall Jackson's Headquarters for 1.1 miles where you will see a cemetery on the left corner. Turn left there, onto Southwerk Street. Take Southwerk past one traffic light and take the next left, Cameron Street. The entrance to Sacred Heart Cemetery, Stop 2, will be on your right, on Bond Street.

After stopping the Confederates at the bottom of the hill, three Union regiments—the 46th Pennsylvania, the 5th Connecticut and the 28th New York—withdrew to this position. There was probably an artillery battery located here too. You may want to visit the cemetery. Photographer Nicholas Routzahn's grave is the first tall obelisk on left near traffic circle.

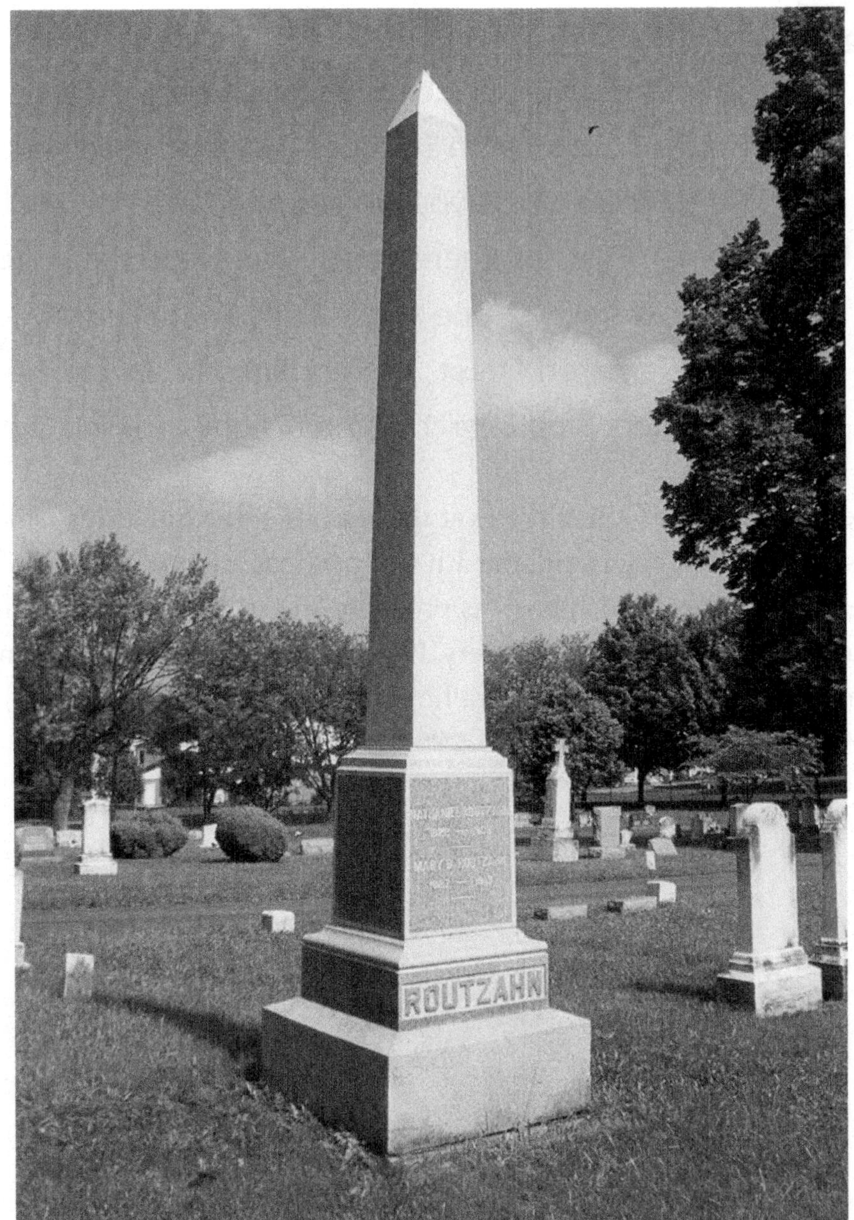

Nicholas Routzahn grave at Sacred Heart Cemetery [Camp Hill]

The cemetery marks the position of the 46th Pennsylvania, supported by the 5th Connecticut and the 28th New York regiments. They held Camp Hill against Ewell's advance while Jackson planned his flank attack from west of the Valley Pike. The cemetery contains the grave of Winchester's Nicholas Routzahn (1822–1908), photographer of the "Crooked Button" portrait. [Bob Price]

STOP 3 OLD MILL TOWN

To reach Stop 3, Old Mill Town, turn left from cemetery. Turn left on Cameron and turn right on Southwerk. At traffic light turn left onto South Loudoun Street. Go south past Jubal Early Drive and cross RR tracks. At the 2nd traffic light, turn right onto Weems Lane. Drive west to intersection with Valley Avenue [Rt. 11]. There is a Burger King on right. Turn right on Valley Avenue and drive short distance. Just before RR crossing turn left into parking area for Virginia Apple Storage Warehouse which is a large red brick building.

Federal resistance on the Valley Pike was just as stiff as on the Millwood Pike. Just to the north, the Federal position stood on better ground, with strong artillery support. The 2nd Massachusetts, 3rd Wisconsin, 29th Pennsylvania and 27th Indiana manned a line on Bowers Hill, just ahead on your left. This line extended to the left or west but Jackson did not know how far. Union artillery firing from the high ground ahead had pinned down his advance on the Valley Pike. Jackson ordered Captain William T. Poague and Captain W.E. Cutshaw to move their cannons forward across Abrams Creek and open fire. However, the Confederate guns were overmatched and soon sharpshooters of the 2nd Massachusetts Infantry began to pick off the gunners.

Captain Joseph Carpenter of the Virginia Artillery described the artillery duel:

> After placing my pieces in position and opening fire . . . I found I was exposed to an enfilading fire from a battery of two pieces on my left and a direct fire from a battery of six pieces in my front. However, after firing some 30 or 40 rounds at the battery to my front, I was very much rejoiced to see it limber to the rear . . . it left me only exposed to the fire of the battery to my left and the enemy's sharpshooters in my rear.

Jackson feared getting his infantry bogged down by the accurate artillery fire and he wanted to avoid the rear guard action of the previous day. He realized that he needed to be aggressive and make something happen.

With the battle hanging in the balance, he called on General Richard Taylor's Louisiana Brigade. One Confederate had described Taylor's men as tigers "in human form. I was actually afraid of them . . . brave desperate fighters." Taylor

Old Mill Town today

Abrams Creek flows just to right of railroad tracks. During the war the creek turned a number of mill wheels in this area collectively called Old Mill Town. The Federals burned the mills before the battle. Early on May 25, Jackson's advance down the Valley Pike ground to a halt here. Union artillery fire from Bowers Hill was severe and accurate. Moreover, four Union infantry regiments—2nd Massachusetts, 3rd Wisconsin, 29th Pennsylvania, and the 27th Indiana—awaited Jackson on the high ground. This area is the likely location of the hurried meeting between generals Jackson, Taylor, and Winder just prior to Taylor's march to the west, along the south bank of the creek. He reached a position to launch the flank attack that won the First Battle of Winchester. [Bob Price]

led his men forward, conferred briefly with Jackson, and then carried out the very first of Stonewall Jackson's flank attacks.

Taylor moved his brigade away from the Valley Pike and marched northwest along Abrams Creek. The swales and the high ground on the right masked his move. There is no marked trail for his route, but we can follow his path in a general way, mindful of Taylor's need to conceal his advance.

STOP 4 SOUTH END OF BOWERS HILL

Leaving Old Mill Town for Stop 4, the first of two for Taylor's attack site, take Valley Avenue north to the second traffic light, and turn left onto Bellview Avenue. You are moving parallel with Taylor's initial advance, which would have been on your left. Go two blocks uphill to intersection with Handley Avenue. Here you may want to pull over at the large boulder on the left and take a look from the intersection. You are at the south end of Bowers Hill. Despite extensive development, the westward view from this corner is still helpful. Taylor's regiments were on the far bank of the creek, off to your left. The column crossed the creek at the bottom of the hill to your front. Then, concealed in a trough-like depression, on his right, Taylor moved up to attack Banks' right flank.

Now, turn left on Handley Avenue and come slowly downhill.

Taylor's Brigade crossed the creek a half mile downhill from the boulder, near the intersection of Handley Avenue and Meadow Branch Avenue and moved northwest. Turn right on Meadow Branch Avenue.

STOP 5 TAYLOR'S ATTACK SITE NEAR TODAY'S MUSEUM OF THE SHENANDOAH VALLEY

Despite all the development here, try to let the terrain tell you what it can. You have high ground on your right. In 1862 it shielded Taylor's Brigade from view as they moved ahead.

After you turn right on Meadow Branch continue past the three way stop. At the second right, turn onto Ramseur Lane. Drive short distance to curve where you may want to pull over for a brief stop. Look toward the water tower and this is the avenue of advance for Taylor's men. The property between the houses and the water tower is owned by the Museum of the Shenandoah Valley.

In the not so distant past, this was a great stop to make—a pristine historical site. Even today, if you lived in one of the houses on the right, you could look out from your backyard and still view the fields over which Taylor's men made the first attack. Today, however, there's no good way to experience the site without cutting through someone's yard—not recommended. A better option will be to continue on to the grounds of the Museum of the Shenandoah Valley, Stop 6.

Taylor's Attack Site

[Bob Price]

Taylor's regiments advanced up the steep ridge in the direction of today's water tower, beyond the crest. Up to this point they had not been seen. Not until the "Tigers" reached the crest and then charged downhill did Union officers see them coming. Their angle of approach to the Union flank was at about 45 degrees. Two Union regiments desperately wheeled their front from the south to the west, but the "Tigers" were on them in the midst of the maneuver. The whole Union line from this point back to Camp Hill quickly collapsed—Taylor had "rolled up" the Union right.

STOP 6 MUSEUM OF THE SHENANDOAH VALLEY [MSV]

To reach the Museum of the Shenandoah Valley [MSV], go to the end of Ramseur Lane. Turn left at the traffic circle onto Mahone Drive. Turn right at Meadow Branch Avenue and go straight to light at Amherst Avenue. Turn right on Amherst and drive 7/10 of a mile east to museum entrance on your right. The Museum (540-662-1473) is closed on Mondays. Here is their website: www.themsv.org

The fields to the south of the museum have not changed since 1862. The left flank of Taylor's Louisiana Brigade attack would have crossed the hills a short distance south of the main museum building. You can walk a short way from the parking lot and imagine the scene on Sunday, May 25, 1862, at about 10 AM. (To go further up hill, inquire at the Museum about permission.) Robert Tanner describes the attack well in his *Stonewall in the Valley* (1996):

> Still mounted, Taylor took his place in front. His lone sabre flashed. Five pelican-bedecked battle flags began to flap. He gave the order and fifteen hundred Louisianans stepped off on the left foot; the 10th and 37th Virginia moved in echelon. A forest of burnished steel paraded against the Union right. Taylor twisted occasionally to check the alignment. It did not falter, though shells chopped and chewed his ranks. Men stepped up to close the gashes. They skirted trees and re-formed, vaulted fences and re-formed, preserving a remarkable elbow-to-elbow formation and absorbing the gaze of hundreds.

Confederate soldier Watkins Kearns wrote in his diary, "Steadily and in unbroken column they advanced through a storm of rifle balls and cannon shot." Henry Kyd Douglas, one of Jackson's staff officers, noted, "I have rarely seen a more beautiful charge. This full brigade, with a line of glistening bayonets bright in that morning sun, its formation straight and compact, its tread quick and easy as it pushed on through the clover and up the hill, was a sight to delight a veteran."

The Union regiments which faced south hastily wheeled to the west, but it was too late. Jackson's first great flank attack struck the Union line at about a 45 degree angle, with 3,000 men. Taylor's men were in full battle cry, with the blue-clad troops at their mercy.

On Taylor's left flank, the 8th Louisiana and Major Chatham R. Wheat's "Tigers" turned back the charge of five companies of the 1st Maine Cavalry, which inflicted serious losses on the horsemen.

Captain Zulich, of the 29th Pennsylvania, described Taylor's attack:

> Before we had got into position we received a volley of musketry from a large body of the enemy to our front, which was not distinctly visible, on account of a fog arising from the damp ground . . . Before we could discern the enemy in front we saw a brigade consisting of four regiments closed en masse on our right flank and rapidly approaching our rear . . . They charged down the hill upon us with deafening cheers . . . We found it impossible to preserve our ranks while climbing up these rocks amidst the fire of the enemy.

General Banks' second in command, General Alpheus Williams, tried to rally his men as the Union front began to crumble in panic. Williams recalled that:

> As we reached the brow of the hill a most terrific fire of infantry was opened upon us from a long line which extended beyond my extreme right . . . The air seemed literally to be full of whizzing bullets, which stirred up currents of air as if the atmosphere had suddenly been filled with some invisible cooling process. The cavalry could do nothing before such an overwhelming force and it went down with great rapidity.

John Worsham, a private in the 21st Virginia, described the charge as: "the grandest I saw during the war; officers, file closers, and every man was in his proper place. There was all the pomp and circumstance of war about it, that was always lacking in our charges, not that it was more effective than those of the old rebel yell, where most of the men would race to be the foremost."

The entire Union position then collapsed as the "Maryland Line" of General Ewell's division stormed into town from the east. In possibly the most uncharacteristic utterance of his life, Jackson shouted, "Very good! Now let's holler!" He raised his gray cap, his staff officers began to cheer, and soon the advancing infantry took up the cheer in a deafening roar.

In town the news of the collapse spread quickly. David Strother, a Virginia (Martinsburg) Unionist and a topographer attached to Banks' staff, was enjoying a cup of coffee and a roll when a soldier came in and said, "They have driven our men off the hill." As Strother assessed the situation the adjutant from the 2nd Massachusetts rode by at a gallop and shouted, "Mount and ride. You have not a minute to lose. They are in the town."

One Confederate soldier recalled, "We took them off the hill and down and through the streets of Winchester." In town he saw "the greatest excitement I saw during the war—the soldiers yelling, the city people, men, women and children yelling—some carrying water . . . we advanced firing as we ran . . ."

As Banks' men retreated through town, they headed for the Martinsburg Pike, today's Route 11 North. Some Winchester citizens shot at them as the Yankees tried to escape. Strother recalled: "As I drew up my horse to within ten steps of a hydrant where some soldiers stopped to drink, I saw the flash of a piece from a gateway and one of the men fell over in the gutter . . ."

One Winchester lady, afraid that too many Yankees would escape, shouted to some Louisiana soldiers, "You are too late—too late!" Whereupon a soldier of the 8th Louisiana gave her a hug and a kiss, and said (in French) "I'm *never* too late!"

The lady was correct because the Yankees had a big head start on their way north. One soldier called it a "big sheduddle." Jackson's infantry couldn't keep up with the Federal refugees. Ashby's cavalry had not rejoined the force since the fight at Buckton Station on May 23.

Jackson pushed ahead with the infantry but only as far as the intersection of Milburn Lane and the Old Charlestown Road in Stephenson. A soldier who saw him there remembered:

> I heard at a distance down the road a loud cheering. We immediately exclaimed, "Old Jack's coming" . . . As he came the men passed in shoals down the road side and waved their hats . . . it was deafening and the tributes of all troops without reference to Division, Brigade, or state. The Louisiana boys were very vociferous. I never saw a more thrilling scene, nor one filled with more interest. General

> Jackson himself seemed much affected as he rode uncovered, bowing constantly.

Most of Banks' troops reached the Potomac River and crossed to safety. Banks would meet Jackson again in August at the Battle of Cedar Mountain. He would also meet Richard Taylor again in the 1864 Red River Campaign in Louisiana.

To return to the Visitors Center from the MSV, return to Amherst Street. Turn right. Follow Amherst Street east until you reach the three way intersection with the traffic light. Bear to your right to merge onto West Boscawen Street. Continue east until you reach the next traffic light. Turn right onto South Stewart Street and continue approximately half a mile until the intersection with Handley Boulevard. Notice Handley High School on your right. Banks' fugitives came streaming down the east side of Bower's Hill, headed for the Valley Pike.

Turn left onto Handley Boulevard and go to the light and turn right onto Valley Avenue. Go past first left and make an immediate left turn into parking lot for a brick building. At corner of Valley and W. Bond Street note the historical marker to the First Battle. If you look to the west you get a good view of Bowers Hill behind the high school.

Turn right out of parking lot and bear right. Go to light [McDonalds on left] and turn right onto Gerrard Street which then becomes Millwood Avenue. Sadly the area around the McDonalds is the location of the last organized Federal resistance. Follow Millwood

Avenue downhill to the intersection where we began our tour. A left turn at the light onto S. Pleasant Valley Avenue brings you back to the entrance to the Visitors Center on the right.

Aftermath
Casualties
First Battle of Winchester

Confederate	*Union*
68 killed	62 killed
329 wounded	243 wounded
3 missing or captured	1,714 missing or captured
Total Confederate Casualties 400	Total Union Casualties 2,019

The casualty figures are from three days of hard fighting and relentless pursuit from Front Royal to Winchester. The high number of Banks' "missing or captured" reveals the impact of Taylor's attack. In addition to the prisoners, Banks left behind 4,354 small arms and 500,000 rounds of ammunition.

The casualty figures would have been higher if Dr. Hunter McGuire had not been on the scene. As the Union troops fled and Confederates rushed into town, several fires broke out. When flames threatened to engulf a military hospital full of sick and wounded men, desperate Union surgeons beseeched McGuire for help. They asked not to be taken prisoner themselves but pleaded for Confederate soldiers to help save their patients' lives. McGuire immediately complied. Later, Jackson approved of McGuire's initiative. Similar arrangements became standard practice for the rest of the war and beyond. Later that day, Lee wrote to Jackson, "I congratulate you upon defeating and then evading your enemy. Your march to Winchester has been of great advantage and has been conducted with your accustomed skill and boldness."

Jackson's success was complete. He had won more than the battle. His successes at Front Royal and Winchester denied General McClellan the reinforcements he (wrongly) believed he needed to take Richmond. Union troops headed to the Peninsula were now redirected to the Valley. But Jackson was not finished. On May 27, he moved north toward Harpers Ferry. When Union forces began to close in on him, he came quickly south, passing through Winchester on May 31. On June 6 he turned on his pursuers, defeating them at Harrisonburg followed by Cross Keys on June 8 and Port Republic the following day. By mid-June he vanished only to reappear with his men near Richmond. General Lee had taken over the command of what he called the Army of Northern Virginia, and Jackson's Valley Army became one wing of that legendary army. Jackson had already become Lee's right arm. What Dr. Charles P. Roland has called "the indomitable team" had been forged in victory.

The victory also forged a bond between Jackson and his "foot cavalry." He earned his men's undying respect and devotion, and he gave them his. One of General Taylor's officers, Captain C. P. Ring, wrote, "I had rather be a private in such an army than a field officer in any other. Jackson is perfectly idolized by this Army, especially this Brigade . . . . He told General Taylor he never saw nor heard of such a charge as was made by us at Winchester . . ."

Order of Battle at First Winchester

May 25, 1862

Confederate

Major General Thomas J. "Stonewall" Jackson

Jackson's Division Major General Charles S. Winder

First (Stonewall) Brigade
- 2nd Virginia Col. J. W. Allen
- 4th Virginia Col. Charles A. Ronald
- 5th Virginia Col. W.S.H. Baylor
- 27th Virginia Col. A.J. Grigsby
- 33rd Virginia Col. John F. Neff

Second Brigade Col. J.A. Campbell
- 21st Virginia Col. John M. Patton
- 42nd Virginia Lt. Col. W. T. Martin
- 48th Virginia Lt. Col. T. S. Garnett

Third Brigade Brigadier General William B. Taliaferro
- 10th Virginia Col. E. T. H. Warren
- 23rd Virginia Col. A.G. Taliaferro
- 37th Virginia Major T.W. Williams

Artillery
- Col. Stapleton Crutchfield

Jackson's Division Artillery
- Carpenter's Battery (Allegheny)
- Caskie's Battery (Hampden)
- Cutshaw's Battery (West Augusta)
- Poague's Battery (Rockbridge)
- Wooding's Battery (Danville)

Ewell's Division Major General Richard Ewell

Scott's Brigade Col. W.C. Scott
- 44th Virginia Major Cobb

52nd Virginia Lt. Col. J.H. Skinner
58th Virginia Col. S. H. Letcher

Elzey's Brigade Brigadier General Arnold M. Elzey
12th Georgia Col. Z.T. Connor
13th Virginia Col. James A. Walker
25th Virginia Lt. Col. Patrick Duffy
31st Virginia Col. John S. Hoffman

Taylor's Brigade Brigadier General Richard S. Taylor
6th Louisiana Col. Isaac G. Seymour
7th Louisiana Col. Harry T. Hayes
8th Louisiana Col. H. B. Kelly
9th Louisiana Col. Leroy A. Stafford
Wheat's Battalion (Louisiana Tigers) Major R.C. Wheat

Trimble's Brigade Major General Isaac C. Trimble
15th Alabama Col. James Cantey
21st Georgia Col. J.T. Mercer
21st North Carolina Col. W.W. Kirkland
16th Mississippi Col. Carnot Posey

Independent
1st Maryland Col. Bradley T. Johnson

Division Artillery

Brockenbrough's Battery
Courtney's Battery (Richmond)
Lusk's Battery (2nd Rockbridge)
Raines' Battery (Lynchburg Lee)
Rice's Battery (8th Star)

Cavalry Col. Turner Ashby
7th Virginia Cavalry Col. Ashby
Brigadier General George H. Steuart
2nd Virginia Cavalry Col. T.T. Munford
6th Virginia Cavalry Col. Thomas Flournoy

Union

Division Commander Brigadier General Alpheus S. Williams

First Brigade Col. Dudley Donnelly
- 5th Connecticut Lt. Col. G.D. Chapman
- 28th New York Lt. Col. E.B. Brown
- 46th Pennsylvania Col. Joseph F. Knipe

Third Brigade Col. G.H. Gordon
- 2nd Massachusetts Lt. Col. George Andrews
- 3rd Wisconsin Col. Thomas H. Ruger
- 27th Indiana Col. Silas T. Colgrove
- 29th Pennsylvania Col. John K. Murphy

Artillery Col. Robert B. Hampton
- Battery M 1st New York Light Artillery Lt. J.H. Peabody
- Battery F Pennsylvania Light Artillery Lt. Presley Fleming
- Battery G 4th U. S. Light Artillery Lt. F.B. Crosby

Cavalry Brigadier General John P. Hatch
- 1st Maine Cavalry (5 cos.) Lt. Col. Calvin R. Douty
- 1st Vermont Cavalry Col. Charles H. Tompkins
- 1st Maryland Cavalry (6 cos.) Lt. Charles Wetschky
- 6th New York cavalry Col. Othnell De Forest

Attached Cavalry
- 1st Michigan Cavalry (8 cos.) Lt. T.F. Brodhead

Attached Commands
- 10th Maine Infantry Col. George L. Beal
- 8th New York Cavalry (8 cos., dismounted) Lt. Col. C.R. Babbitt
- Battery E Pennsylvania Artillery Lt. Col. C.M. Atwell
- Pennsylvania Zoauves d'Afrique Captain Charles H.T. Collis

CHAPTER 3

THE SECOND BATTLE OF WINCHESTER

JUNE 14–15, 1863

WILBUR NYE, IN HIS BOOK, *Here Come the Rebels,* called the summer of 1863 the most dramatic summer in American history. The drama unfolded across the South: on the Mississippi River, in middle Tennessee, and from Virginia to Pennsylvania. Early in May, Lee's Army of Northern Virginia won its greatest victory, at Chancellorsville. The victory gave Lee the strategic initiative, and he seized this advantage by crossing the Potomac River again.

> Because the Forks of the Shenandoah River and the main stem Shenandoah River flow from south to north, military movement in the Valley from south to north is called "down" the Valley and movement from north to south is "up" the Valley. This is why the area around Winchester is known as the Lower Valley and the area southwest near Staunton is known as the Upper Valley. Failure to understand this will result in confusion.

In 1862, after the victory at Second Manassas, Lee had crossed the Potomac near Leesburg, Virginia, east of the Blue Ridge Mountains and fought at South Mountain and Sharpsburg. In 1863, he moved west of the mountains and marched down the Valley directly through Winchester.

The year between Jackson's victory at the First Battle of Winchester and his death after the Battle of Chancellorsville had been hard on Winchester's residents and its infrastructure. Quickly reoccupied after Jackson left the Valley in June 1862, the town began to show the ravages and strains of what was becoming a long war. Winchester's fate had troubled Jackson. In a letter to Senator Alexander Boteler he wrote:

> Though I have been relieved from command there I feel deeply when I see the patriotic people of that region again under the heel of a hateful military despotism . . . there are those who have so devotedly labored for the relief of our suffering, sick, and wounded soldiers.

The fate of Senator James Mason's Winchester house, Selma, is an apt symbol of the war grinding on—and also the dawning of emancipation. Mason had been the author of the Fugitive Slave Act, part of the Compromise of 1850. General Banks, a fervent abolitionist, had ordered the house destroyed. In a letter to his daughter Mildred, General Lee sadly noted that:

> Poor Winchester has been terribly devastated and the inhabitants plundered of all they possessed. Mr. James Mason's residence [*"Selma" on Amherst Street*] has been torn down to the ground. Scarcely one brick stands upon another and a pile of rubbish rests upon the hill on which it stood.

Winchester began the year of 1863 under a new master, Union general Robert H. Milroy. Though not a professional soldier, Milroy had some military experience. He had served with the 1st Indiana Volunteers in 1846–47, during the Mexican-American War. However, Milroy was a lawyer by training and when war came he left behind his law practice in Rennselaer, Indiana, to become a captain in the 9th Indiana. By the time he came to Winchester on January 1, he had been promoted to brigadier general due to combat experience he had received at the battles of McDowell, Cross Keys, and Second Manassas. He was brave and aggressive, although his record included no striking successes, and one bloody repulse at Manassas. He had scant respect for West Point officers.

General Robert H. Milroy (1816–1890)

General Milroy commanded the Union garrison of Winchester in the Second Battle. A court of inquiry exonerated him of blame for the defeat. Professor Jonathan Noyalas, Director of the Center for Civil War History at Lord Fairfax Community College, has written a modern (2006) well balanced biography of Milroy, "My Will Is Absolute Law." *[Library of Congress]*

Like Banks, Milroy was committed to abolition long before the Emancipation Proclamation. He had even adopted one runaway slave, whom he named Benjamin Summit (for Cheat Mountain Summit, where Ben came to him seeking refuge). When Milroy came to Winchester in January 1863 he came with the power of the Emancipation Proclamation behind him. On January 5, he issued his own proclamation in Winchester that he titled "Freedom to Slaves." As he worked to strengthen Winchester's fortifications, he saw to it that the few remaining foundation blocks from Selma went into the gun emplacements at Star Fort, just north of town. He saw himself as a latter-day Moses, leading the slaves out of a latter-day Egypt, thus his assignment to Winchester became part of his divine/moral mission to enforce the Emancipation Proclamation. However, his fervor blinded him to some dangerous military realities.

Milroy's garrison in Winchester comprised about 7,400 men in the three brigades led by Brigadier General Washington Elliott, Colonel William Ely, and Colonel Andrew McReynolds. (From April 1863 forward, McReynolds' brigade was posted in Berryville)

Winchester was a garrison post in Major General Robert Schenck's Middle Department, erected to protect the line of the Baltimore & Ohio Railroad from raiders and partisans. While Winchester's garrison was the largest in the Department there were concerns in Washington that Milroy's position at Winchester was too far south to protect the railroad while leaving his troops vulnerable to attack. Milroy did not share either concern because he believed that his men could protect the railroad and attack Confederates in the Lower Shenandoah Valley.

Ruling Winchester with a dictatorial hand and enforcing emancipation, he meant to break the spirit of Winchester's Confederate citizens and rally the few Unionists. His name became infamous in Winchester, and throughout Virginia. The Confederate Congress labeled him as an outlaw. The resentment toward the Union officer lingers even to this day, thanks to Milroy's policy of exile for several hundred uncooperative Winchester citizens along with confiscation of their homes and other private property.

For this reason the title of Jonathan Noyalas' biography of Milroy—*"My Will is Absolute Law"* is well chosen.

The best known example of exile and confiscation was the sad case of Mrs. Lloyd Logan and her daughters. Milroy had made his headquarters in their house. In April, when Mrs. Milroy came to Winchester, Mrs. Logan and her daughters, one of whom was severely ill, were bundled out of town, never to return.

Milroy overestimated the strength of Union sentiment in Winchester along with his own military strength. He had great faith in his three fortified (earthwork) positions: Fort Milroy, Star Fort, and West Fort. Fort Milroy (also known as Flag Fort, Milroy's Fort, Main Fort, and Fort Garabaldi) was just north of the center of town. In his excellent study, *Gateway to Gettysburg* (2003), Larry Maier calculated that the four 20-pound Parrott guns of the 14th Massachusetts Heavy Artillery, located in Fort Milroy, had an effective range of about 1,300 yards which was enough to reach the southern edge of town. Star Fort, Milroy's pride, stood about a half-mile northeast of Fort Milroy.

Star Fort was built on the site of a Confederate position, Fort Alabama. Star-shaped forts, with five diamond shaped gun emplacements originated in late medieval Europe. Michelangelo designed some of the first for the city of Florence. Noyalas' study of Milroy's notebooks from his student years at the Norwich Military Academy show that the young Milroy was much taken with the design. He took great pride in all his Winchester fortifications, but especially Star Fort. The Star Fort site has been recently restored by the Shenandoah Valley Battlefields Association.

West Fort and several smaller positions were about a half-mile west of Star Fort. West Fort was the weakest of the three, but there seemed to be no reason to expect trouble from the north or west. In addition, a line of rifle pits ran from Fort Milroy south to Bowers Hill. His men had cleared away all the timber and vegetation from these and other battery positions, creating wide fields of fire for Milroy's powerful artillery complement.

Milroy's officers and men admired him and they presented him with two different swords celebrating the occupation of Winchester which reinforced his belief in the righteousness of his mission and the strength of his position. He did not believe, later rumors and scouting reports to the contrary, that Winchester would ever be in the sights of a significant portion of the Army of Northern Virginia.

In May 1863, the Army of Northern Virginia achieved a great victory at Chancellorsville, but it suffered a great loss in the death of Stonewall Jackson. The loss of Jackson had incalculable results. Unwilling to name a successor to lead Jackson's wing of the army, Lee decided to reorganize it. Two wings became three corps. To command the Second Corps, Lee named Jackson's subordinate at First Winchester, General Richard S. Ewell.

Unlike Milroy, Ewell was a professional soldier with a long and distinguished record. Like Milroy, he too had strong feelings about slavery. Bruce Levine, in *Confederate Emancipation* (2008), points out that in 1861, just after the Battle of Manassas, Ewell made a radical and forthright proposal to President Davis to augment Confederate manpower by "emancipating and arming the slaves." Davis immediately dismissed the idea.

At the Battle of Second Manassas (Groveton) in August 1862, Ewell was severely wounded. Winchester's Dr. McGuire amputated his leg. Ewell's recovery was long and painful. He did not return to the Army until named to command the Second Corps. Fitted with a wooden leg, he could ride horseback but generally traveled in a carriage.

By the time of the Second Battle of Winchester, Richard Ewell was almost a new man. He had a new leg; he was newly married; and he had been newly promoted to lieutenant general in command of an army corps. He was fortunate that his three division commanders: Jubal Early, Edward Johnson and Robert Rodes were all capable and experienced soldiers.

General Richard S. Ewell (1817–1872)

General Richard S. Ewell led a division under Jackson in the First Battle of Winchester. After Jackson's death he became commander of the Second Corps in 1863. [Library of Congress]

As for Lee, he had lost Jackson, but he had won the strategic initiative. Believing that the passage of time only favored the North, he determined to force the issue and cross the Potomac, west of the Blue Ridge. Ewell's corps would the lead the way down the Valley, through Winchester. Taking Winchester was a necessity—to open a line of communication and supply for the invasion. Lee believed that Milroy's Union troops would evacuate the town, but if they remained—then opportunity joined necessity—the opportunity to destroy an entire Federal division and its infamous commander.

On June 3, Lee began his move west from Fredericksburg, toward the Valley. The First (Longstreet's) and Second Corps reached Culpeper Court House on June 8. Following the cavalry clash at Brandy Station on June 9, Ewell's corps headed for the Lower Valley the next day.

Rumors and reports of a possible, even likely, Confederate move toward Winchester soon reached Milroy, but he gave them no credence. He did send his sick and wounded north on June 10, but he remained confident he could hold Winchester against virtually any Confederate force. In Washington, his superiors vacillated. On June 12, Schenck, in Baltimore, ordered him to be ready to pull out, but also to hold his ground. That same day, Ewell came through Chester Gap into the Valley, headed for Front Royal. After a warm welcome there, he divided the corps for the next phase. He sent Rode's division on to Berryville, to drive out or capture McReynolds' brigade and then move on to Martinsburg. (McReynolds would escape and come into Winchester on the 13th). Johnson's men headed for Winchester via the Front Royal Pike, while Early moved down the Valley Pike.

Reports of the Confederate advance soon inundated Milroy. He sent out strong patrols accompanied by artillery along both pikes. At Middletown, a detachment of Confederate cavalry was lured into an ambush on the Valley Pike. The Union force then withdrew to Kernstown. Heavier fighting followed the next day on June 13. From Pritchard's Hill the Federals clearly saw the magnitude of the threat.

A Federal soldier remembered:

> I saw a scout coming, almost flying down the pike. Jumped his horse over a stone fence that surrounded our camp, headed straight for the Colonel's tent. Without any ceremony rushed in . . . Fall in, fall in, double quick . . . we were in a bad fix, as we could see the gray in all directions . . .

Early pushed the Federals from Kernstown to the Cedar Creek Grade and then to Abrams Creek. To cover his withdrawal to the north bank, Brigadier General Washington Elliott launched a counterattack with the 123rd Ohio, and the 12th West Virginia. Union captain John Carlin's 1st West Virginia Battery inflicted heavy casualties in John Gordon's brigade. The 12th Pennsylvania Cavalry charged up the Pike, moving straight for the 9th Louisiana, which drove them back with heavy losses.

Elliott's brigade soon reached the safety of Abram's Creek's north bank. There was no further pursuit. The determining factor was the accurate artillery fire of the heavy guns from Fort Milroy. Lieutenant Colonel Hilary P. Jones, commanding the artillery battalion in Early's division, reported that his guns lacked the range to reach Fort Milroy. Therefore, even though Johnson's division had not been engaged, Ewell called a halt.

That night a storm raged and its high winds brought down the telegraph line to Harpers Ferry. The following morning, June 14, dawned clear and bright. At first light pickets from Gordon's brigade moved cautiously toward the summit of Bowers Hill. They found only a few Federal pickets. The fighting soon moved into town. A Georgian wrote, "We were joined by six or eight little boys from ten to fourteen years of age armed with shotguns and every imaginable weapon . . . they fought like wild cats and could get at the Yankees better than we could."

At about 9:00 AM, Ewell and Early rode up to a good vantage point on Bowers Hill. It was clear that an assault on the big forts would be costly, but the view out to the north and northwest seemed promising. High ground west of town offered a way to bypass Fort Milroy and Star Fort. A flanking column could march north and then attack West Fort from the west. The attack would come from an unexpected direction. Ewell believed that Milroy might evacuate Winchester if West Fort fell. Flank marches were difficult and dangerous operations, but Ewell believed that he might be successful if he utilized his entire battalion of artillery. The march would be between eight and ten miles, and there was no time to lose. The stage was set as Ewell issued the necessary orders to begin the Second Battle of Winchester.

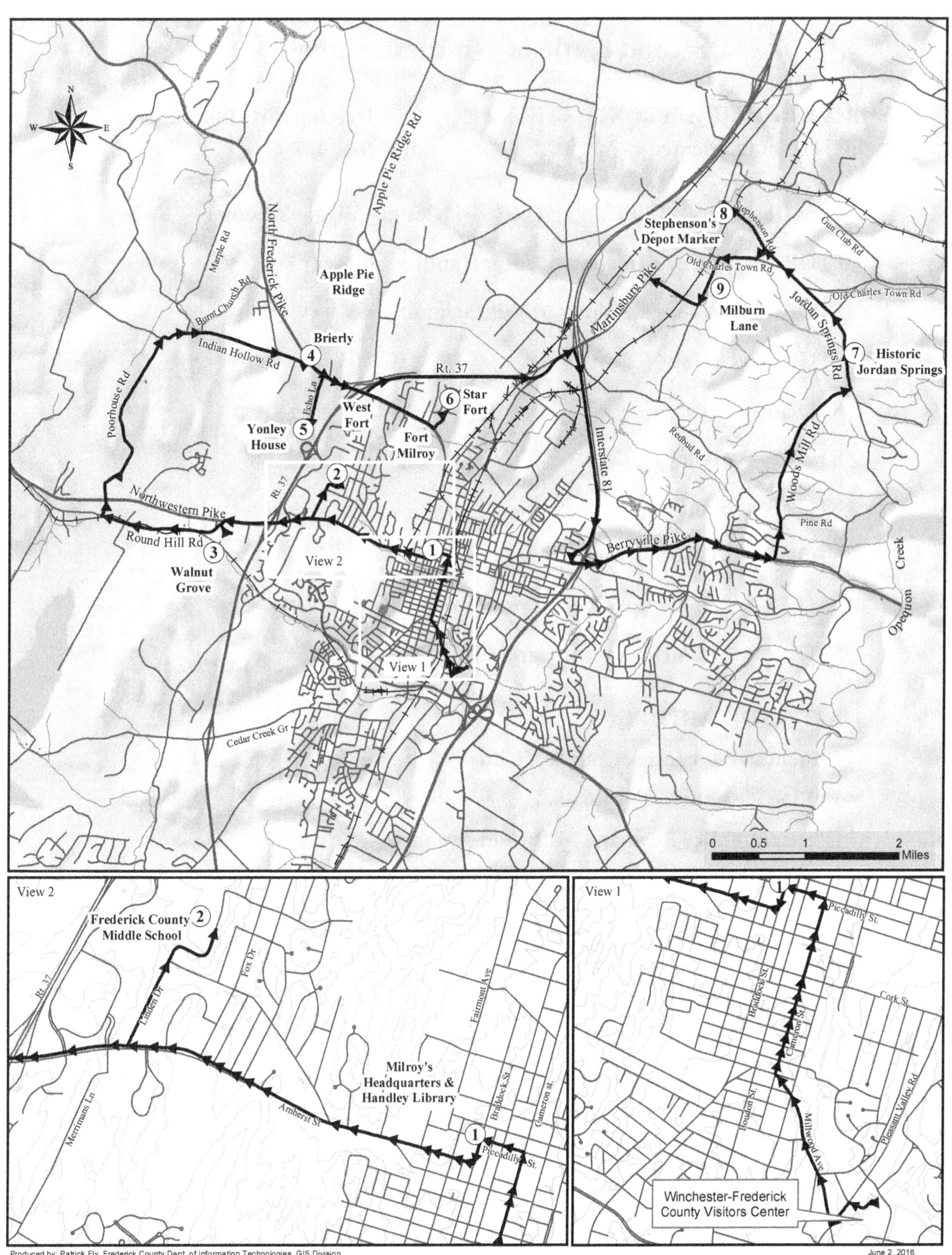

Second Battle of Winchester, June 14–15, 1863

Second Battle of Winchester Tour

DRIVING TIME APPROXIMATELY 2 HOURS—Driving directions are sans serif and indented

Point of Departure—Winchester-Frederick County Visitor's Center

STOP 1 Milroy's Headquarters & Handley Library

STOP 2 Frederick County Middle School

STOP 3 Walnut Grove

STOP 4 Brierly

STOP 5 Yonley House

STOP 6 Star Fort

STOP 7 Jordan Springs

STOP 8 Stephenson's Depot Monument and Marker

STOP 9 Milburn Lane, or Carter's Woods

POINT OF DEPARTURE:

Winchester-Frederick County Visitor's Center

1400 S. Pleasant Valley Road

(Pleasant Valley Road and Millwood Avenue)

Open daily 9:00–5:00

The Winchester-Frederick County Civil War Orientation Center provides background for all local Civil War history. The telephone number is (540) 542-1326 or toll free (877) 871-1326

www.visitwinchesterva.com/civil-war-orientation-center

STOP 1 MILROY'S HEADQUARTERS & HANDLEY LIBRARY

To reach Stop 1, Milroy's Headquarters and the Handley Library leave the Visitors Center and turn left on S. Pleasant Valley Avenue. Turn right at the light onto Millwood Avenue. Cross the RR tracks and go to 2nd right turn and head north on S. Cameron Street. Go through numerous intersections and look for historic George Washington Hotel on right. At that intersection turn left onto East Piccadilly Street. At the second light, Braddock Street, turn left and seek parking if you wish to take a closer look at these buildings. The Logan House is the large brick building with the large red apple in front. Milroy used this house as his headquarters. The Handley Library is across the street.

The Logan House

The Logan House was Milroy's headquarters in 1863 and General Phillip Sheridan's in 1864. [John Fox]

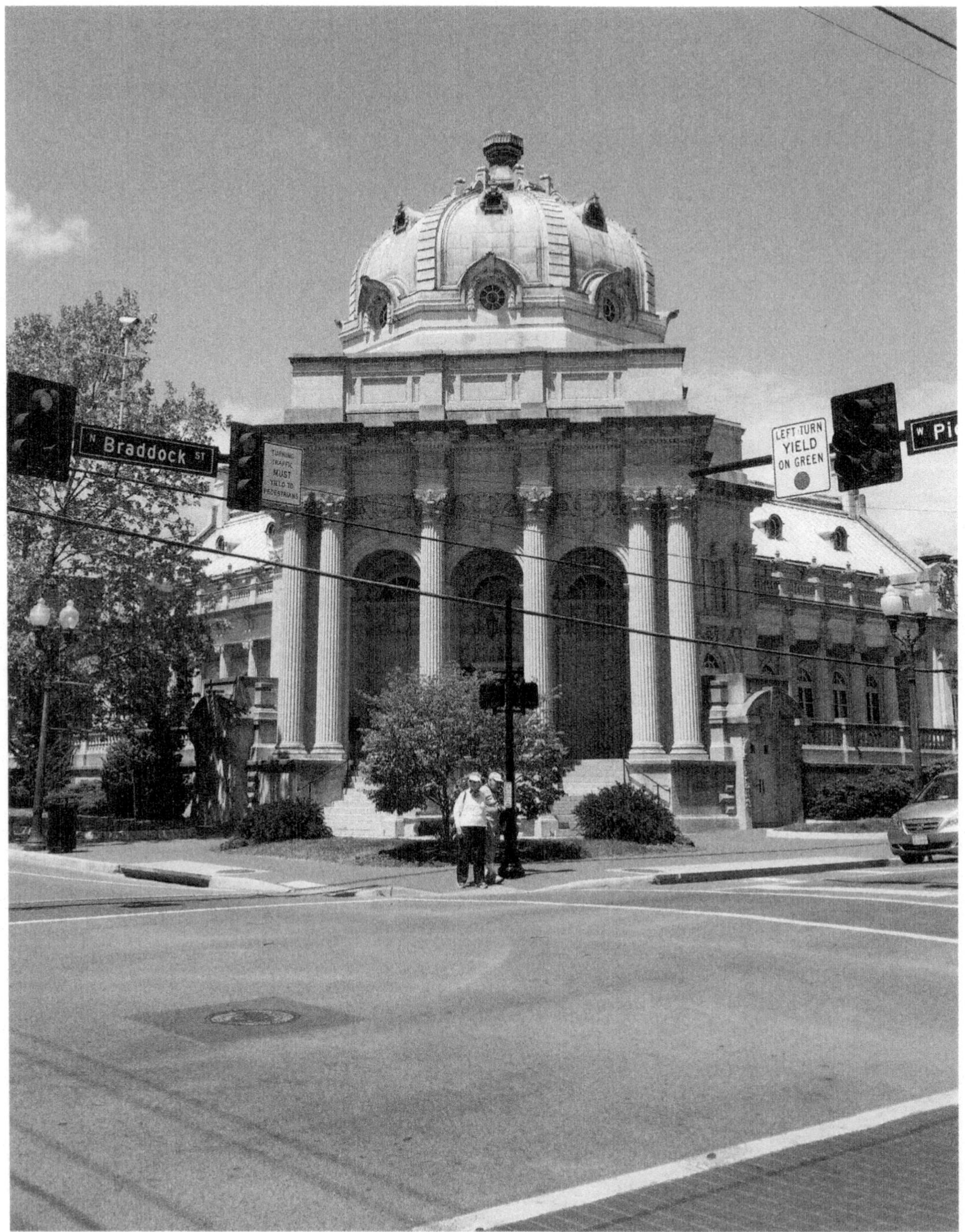

The Handley Library

The Library's founder, Judge John Handley (1835–1895) came to America from Ireland in 1854 and soon took up residence in Scranton, Pa. He married a Southerner, from Charleston, S.C. When war came he served briefly in a militia unit, but seems to have been a Confederate sympathizer.

He was a frequent visitor to Winchester after the war. Although he died in Scranton he is buried here, in the Mt. Hebron Cemetery, a few yards from the Stonewall Confederate Cemetery, under a memorial he designed himself. He left $250,000 for a library in Winchester, and what amounted to $1,250,000 for a school—Handley High School. [John Fox]

To reach our next stop, the Frederick County Middle School, continue south on Braddock Street to the next right, Amherst Street. The McGuire House [home of Dr. Hunter McGuire] is on the corner. Turn right and follow Amherst for about ½ mile. At the corner of Hawthorne Drive, the Hawthorne House is the white home uphill on the right. Hawthorne was the home of the Confederate diarist, Cornelia McDonald. She and Milroy clashed frequently, an entertaining story Jonathan Noyalas tells in his Milroy biography, *My Will is Absolute Law.* You may want to turn right for a better look at the house. If you do, the street loops around uphill and brings you back to Amherst Street.

As Early formed his men up for their long march, the Confederate artillery opened fire on Fort Milroy. Federal guns answered, setting off an artillery duel that put Hawthorne in a dangerous position.

Cornelia McDonald wrote: "We are together in the dining room looking to the West; and it seems strange to sit quietly in a rocking chair and watch the progress of a battle . . . on that sweet June morning."

STOP 2 FREDERICK COUNTY MIDDLE SCHOOL

After passing Hawthorne, continue west 9/10 mile on Amherst Street until Linden Drive [just before light]. Turn right, and follow it uphill into the parking lot of Frederick County Middle School. At the southern end of the parking lot there is a good vantage point to look west over the terrain and direction of Early's march.

Although Milroy did not expect an attack from the west he did try to guard himself against one. He sent a cavalry patrol out to the west and then reinforced the West Fort garrison with two guns and some infantry.

Early was confident that his attack would succeed, but his march carried several difficulties. He needed to ensure that the column remained concealed plus the route needed to be relatively level. They also needed a guide to keep the troops from making a wrong turn. At our next stop, Walnut Grove, Early found his first guide.

STOP 3 WALNUT GROVE

To reach Stop 3, Walnut Grove, return to Amherst Street and turn right. Drive west 1 mile. At the traffic light turn left onto Rt. 803, Round Hill Road. After 1/4 mile, a gravel driveway, on the right, leads to Walnut Grove, 324 Round Hill Road. Park on the left side of the road. The owner requests that you not drive down, but you are welcome to walk down for a look at the house.

Walnut Grove

The owner, John Stevens, requests that you walk rather than drive to view the house. Stevens is a long time board member of the Fort Collier Civil War Center. Jubal Early stopped here on June 14 on his march to West Fort. The core of the house dates from the 18th century. [John Fox]

Early found what he needed at Walnut Grove, which was guide help from "a wealthy and intelligent citizen, whose name I forebear to mention as he has already been subject to the enemy's persecution." Union troops had earlier discovered that the home's owner, Dr. Lupton, had been hoarding corn in his attic for Confederate troops. A sharp-eyed Union officer had spotted a number of squirrels moving in and out of the attic and after a brief search he found and confiscated the corn. Later, when Jubal Early arrived, Lupton was eager to help direct Confederate troops on a concealed path to the north.

The way to West Fort led along a narrow valley floor that today has cultivated fields and orchards. The next part of our ride, as we parallel Early's route to Stop 4, "Brierly" takes us through Frederick County's most beautiful and unspoiled countryside.

STOP 4 BRIERLY

To reach Stop 4, continue west on Round Hill Road. After the 2nd RR crossing turn right onto Rt 654 [Poorhouse Rd]. Cross over Rt. 50 and continue straight along Rt. 654. At the top of the hill, depending on the season, you can look out to the right [east] and clearly see the water tower on Bowers Hill. Continue on 654 to a stop sign. Turn right on Rt 679 [Indian Hollow Rd] and drive uphill. After a half mile the road passes Rosedale, a large house uphill on the left.

Distant water tower on Bowers Hill

[John Fox]

Built in 1781, Rosedale was the home of Joseph C. Baker (1762–1833). Baker raised peaches on this 1,500 acre farm. If you look uphill you can see his pyramid shaped tomb. A dubious legend has it that he chose the location as a permanent visual warning to his slaves—don't steal the produce! At the time of the war his sons, Edwin and Colonel Robert Baker lived here, raising livestock.

Thomas K. Cartmell, author of *Shenandoah Valley Pioneers and Their Descendants . . .* 1738–1908 speaks eloquently of Joseph Baker's tomb:

> " . . . its occupant had dreams of eternal durability . . . but we find now, after a lapse of 75 years only, that what was then regarded impossible, shows marks of gradual ruin. Another cycle of time may find the old monument a confused mess, with the great stones tumbled in upon the dust of the eccentric old occupant."

Continue on through the small community of Albin, formerly Brierly. Bear right beyond the stop sign. About a 1/4 mile later near the end of the road you'll see the Virginia Fruit Market on the left. Turn into the parking area and go to the Virginia Trails sign. Face the sign and note the treetops in distance that stand on the site of West Fort. Look to the right of the sign and note the ridge behind the Winchester Equipment Company. This is the area where Early's troops formed before the attack against West Fort.

West Fort area in distance beyond power lines

[John Fox]

Ridge west of West Fort

The area to the right of the historical marker is where Early's troops formed into line of battle in preparation for their assault.

Early ended his march here. He had stolen a march on the enemy and had West Fort at his mercy. A Confederate soldier, Bartlett Yancey Malone summed it up: ". . . moved around to the west of Winchester taken 20 peases of artillery with us and when we got opersit the Yankees with the artillery taken this position . . ."

The position on the ridge is directly in front of you and to the right. In 1863, as today, the ridge fronted an orchard. Lt. Colonel Hilary P. Jones deployed his guns just behind the ridge. He divided the guns into two groups, one of 12 and the other of 8 guns, to put West Fort in a crossfire. General Harry Hays' Louisiana Tigers—the men who had taken Bowers Hill for Jackson in 1862—would make the attack across the narrow valley and up the slopes of West Fort.

Defending the fort were infantrymen from the 110th and 116th Ohio. There were also artillerists from the 5th U.S. Artillery who manned eight guns in the fort and two more in a smaller work on the other side of the Pughtown Road (today's Rt. 522).

Early and Hays crept forward for a better look through their field glasses. In West Fort, the Federal occupants seemed to be focused in the opposite direction toward Winchester, where intermittent artillery fire continued. Satisfied with the stealth of their march they returned to the ridge. Hays aligned his five regiments. When all was ready, at about 6:00 PM, Early ordered Jones to roll his guns up to the crest and open fire.

A Louisiana soldier revealed "the rapid and well-directed fire upon the redoubt, some of the shells exploding in the work, while others struck the parapet, making great holes in it, sending the dirt high up in the air." Bartlett Yancey Malone noted: ". . . our Baterys opend on them taken them on surprise . . . charged on them and taken their first line of brest works before nite."

Hays went forward with his men. Early had instructed him to halt just before he came within view from the Fort. At that point Jones would halt the artillery fire. However, the attack was difficult to coordinate. Hays halted, but the guns continued firing. Hays then ordered his men to charge across open ground under friendly cannon fire. The Yonley House, which is our next stop, stood directly in the Louisiana Tigers' path.

STOP 5 YONLEY HOUSE

Turn right on North Frederick Pike [Rt. 522] and after a few yards, right on Echo Lane. This is Fruit Hill Orchards property, but we are welcome here. (There is orchard traffic on the lane, so be careful). The Yonley house is directly ahead.

Yonley House

This was the residence of Alma and Lizzie Yonley, who cared for soldiers from the 6th Louisiana regiment shot down in their yard. [Bob Price]

The inhabitants, Lizzie and Alma Yonley had moved here as refugees from Hampshire County in western Virginia early in the war. Now their new home was in the middle of a battlefield, with five regiments of screaming Tigers charging through the yard while dead and wounded lay scattered around the house.

Terry Jones, in *Lee's Tigers* (1987) cites Lizzie Yonley's recollection of the scene: "with banners flying and our men and the enemy's shells flying over . . . the storming of those breastworks was the grandest sight my eyes ever beheld."

The Tigers were intent on winning their second battle of Winchester in thirteen months. However, they found the fight for West Fort harder than the previous year's fight for Bowers Hill. One Confederate soldier recalled:

> The Yankee artillerymen, who were regulars, strove hard to save their guns, but by shooting the horses, we prevented them from taking away a single piece or caisson . . . but took few prisoners, the Yanks being too nimble afoot for us . . . Adjutant John Orr of the

> 6th Regiment seeing a Yankee colorbearer with a guard of two men carrying off his flag ran to him to secure it; overtaking them, Orr seized the standard and with his sword singlehanded commenced a fight . . . but they were too many for him and after a short contest Orr was run through the body with a bayonet and the flag carried away. Strange to say he recovered from his wound.

Killing the artillery horses ended the fight. With the guns immobile the Ohio troops abandoned the fort and escaped to Star Fort. It had been a hard fight. Hays lost 12 men killed and 67 wounded. Among the near casualties was Ewell. Watching from afar through field glasses, a spent bullet from somewhere hit him square in the chest, knocking him to the ground. (Sixteen days later, in the streets of Gettysburg, he would be hit again, by a "live" bullet, but in his wooden leg).

When Early saw that the Tigers held the fort, he rushed up some of Jones' guns and they sighted the captured guns on Star Fort. Within minutes, the new Confederate artillery post, West Fort, opened fire on Star Fort.

STOP 6 STAR FORT

To reach Star Fort, Stop 6, return to North Frederick Pike [Rt. 522] and turn right toward Winchester. Just under a mile after the Rt. 37 overpass turn left on Fortress Drive in front of the red brick Red Cross building. Drive uphill to the entrance of the Fort on the right.

Outside wall of Star Fort

[John Fox]

Star Fort looking toward West Fort in distant treeline

[John Fox]

Milroy had built this fort on the site of an earlier Confederate post, Fort Alabama. The battery assigned here in June 1863, was Captain Frederick Alexander's Baltimore Light Artillery while Colonel Andrew T. McReynolds' infantry brigade manned the rifle pits. Alexander had schooled his gun crews well. They had the exact range of West Fort and got the better of the duel with the guns in West Fort. But that duel touched off a tremendous barrage all across Winchester, from Bowers Hill to Fort Milroy. Gunners on both sides loaded shot and shell, and the flash of deafening reports lit up the evening sky.

It was a spectacular show. Mrs. McDonald watched and listened from Hawthorne, and she later wrote, "Then it seemed as if shells and cannon balls poured from every direction at once . . . horses wounded and bleeding, and men wounded also, and pale with fright. More artillery and more horses and pale flying men rush by where I stood."

Later, as darkness approached, she described seeing General Milroy:

> General Milroy with a few of his body guard galloped by; I saw his pale agitated face as he passed within ten feet of me . . . I bowed to him . . . he bowed low, till his plume almost touched his horse's mane. The fort all the time was sending its huge shot and shell over and through the town . . . from the west proceeded a blaze of fire and a cloud of smoke that carried death into their stronghold into which they were crowding by the hundreds.

Mrs. Mary Greenhow Lee described the scene as "a magnificent sight; every moment the red glare, the deep sound of the heavy siege guns, and the sharper report of our artillery."

Some have questioned whether there was a night attack on Star Fort. Larry Maier, in *Gateway to Gettysburg* pointed to some Union sources who stated that there was a night attack and that it was repulsed. Confederate sources failed to mention such an attack. A Confederate night assault on Star Fort seemed unlikely because the whole purpose of Early's long march to Brierly had been to avoid such an assault even in the daylight.

At about 9:00 PM, Milroy decided to evacuate the forts and "cut our way out" as he put it. His only way out was a move north on the Martinsburg Pike (Rt. 11 N). It is unclear whether he knew that Robert Rodes' Confederate division was at Martinsburg or that Edward Johnson's division was east of Winchester and that either command might be able to cut off his retreat northeast toward Harper's Ferry.

Evacuating the forts and forming the Union column on the Martinsburg Pike took a long time, perhaps three hours, and it had to be done quietly. The gunners spiked their cannons. Word soon spread through Winchester that the Federals were pulling out. The column began to "grow" a long trail of non-combatant refugees—sutlers, teamsters, the officers' wives, and a number of free black refugees. The withdrawal had to be done under the noses of the Confederates in West Fort. As Larry Maier points out, if the column could have departed even an hour earlier, the outcome on June 15th might have been much different. Ewell sensed that Milroy might sacrifice his forts to try to save his command so he moved to block the route to Harpers Ferry—but just barely in time.

He ordered Johnson's division, inactive all day on the Berryville Pike east of Winchester to find a blocking position on the Martinsburg Pike north of town. It meant a difficult night's march for Johnson, as difficult as Early's march in the afternoon. Johnson took the three brigades of George Steuart, Francis Nicholls, and James Walker's Stonewall Brigade. He also took eight guns from Lt. Richard Snowden Andrews' battalion. Like Early, Johnson would need hard marching, some luck and a guide. He found the guide he needed at our next stop, Jordan Springs.

STOP 7 JORDAN SPRINGS

To reach Stop 7, Jordan Springs, leave Star Fort and turn right on North Frederick Pike/Rt. 522 North. Drive to the Rt. 37 interchange and take Rt. 37 North to Interstate 81. As you approach Interstate 81 take entrance ramp for I-81 South. Drive south to next exit, exit 315. At end of exit ramp, turn left onto Rt. 7 East [Berryville Avenue] and drive east towards Berryville. Drive 2 miles and get in left lane for left exit and take the median crossover onto Wood's Mill Road [Rt. 660]. Follow it to its T-intersection with Jordan Springs Road

[Rt. 664]. Turn left and when you go downhill look for the entrance to Jordan Springs on the left.

Jordan Springs

The present structure was built in 1893 while an earlier building, known as Jordan's White Sulphur Springs Resort, dates from 1832. The building that Brigadier General Edward Johnson visited the night of June 14, 1863, was built in 1855 and burned some time in the 1880s. The present building has been the Holy Trinity Mission Seminary and is now the Historic Jordan Springs Event & Cultural Center. [Bob Price]

Jordan Springs was the site of Jordan's White Sulphur Springs Resort. Johnson stopped here well before first light on June 15. At the resort he found the guide he needed, the innkeeper named Edwin Clarendon Jordan, Sr. Jordan either described or personally led Johnson to the intersection of the Martinsburg Pike and the Old Charles Town Road, several miles west of the hotel. Just east of this intersection a narrow bridge carried the Old Charles Town Road over the tracks of the Winchester & Harpers Ferry Railroad. The railroad ran parallel to the Pike; the bridge was about a half-mile south of the depot at Stephenson.

STOP 8

STEPHENSON'S DEPOT MONUMENT AND MARKER

To reach Stop 8, the Stephenson's Depot Marker and Monument, leave Jordan Springs, turning left. Follow Jordan Springs Road [Rt 664] to a fork. Bear right on Stephenson Road [Rt. 664]. The site of the depot was on the left at the railroad crossing. Martinsburg Pike [Rt. 11 north] is just ahead. The monument and marker are in the churchyard of the Emmanuel United Methodist Church on the left, 2732 Martinsburg Pike.

Stephenson's Depot Monument

It is one of only two monuments erected on any of Winchester's battlefields. The other is the small monument to Captain Hastings erected near Ft. Collier [see Ch. 4]. [Bob Price]

The tablet on the boulder depicts the fighting on the bridge, our next stop. In 1920 the descendants of Confederate artillerists Richard Snowden Andrews and J. V. Owens dedicated the monument on land donated by Ray Stephenson. The boulder, tablet and pedestal are all the work of Bryant Percy Baker (1881–1970). Baker came to America from England in 1916. He served in a medical unit in World War I, designing artificial limbs and face masks for soldiers. His best known work is "Pioneer Woman," 1938, in Ponce City, Oklahoma. The tablet on the boulder here depicts two guns from Andrews' battalion holding the bridge against repeated assaults by troops of Elliott's brigade. The bridge was the focal point in the battle of Stephenson's Depot, or Carter's Woods.

The historical analogy on the tablet is incorrect because the Spartans died in an *un*successful attempt to hold the pass at Thermopylae. The Confederates, of course, held the bridge here. Also, General Lee is unlikely to have said what is attributed to him on the monument.

Stephenson Depot Monument Unveiling

The scene of the unveiling in 1920. Sad to say no one in the photograph is identified. The group left of center may be Confederate veterans. [Handley Library Collection, Stewart Bell, Jr. Archives Room, Handley Regional Library, Winchester, VA]

STOP 9 MILBURN LANE OR CARTER'S WOODS

To reach the scene of the fighting Baker depicted, return to the railroad crossing, cross the tracks and take the first right, Gun Club Road. Follow it to Old Charles Town Road [Rt. 761] and turn right. Just past the entrance to Snowden Bridge subdivision turn left onto unpaved Milburn Road [Rt. 662]. Stop at the Virginia Civil War Trails marker on the right. You may want to walk near the bridge on Old Charles Town Road, but be very careful as there is no shoulder near the bridge and lots of traffic.

Old Charles Town Road bridge over RR.

The road today crosses over the railroad at the same location as the war-time bridge. [John Fox]

Milburn Road and marker facing south

[John Fox]

You are now at the center of the battle depicted on the monument—Milburn Road runs parallel with:

a. the ridge behind you

b. the railroad

c. Carter's Woods, now gone, between the railroad and the Pike

d. The Pike, along which Milroy's columns were heading north.

Johnson and his staff crossed the bridge and neared the intersection with the Martinsburg Pike. He stopped just ahead of the Union vanguard of Elliott's brigade. Johnson wrote that he could see nothing in the dark: "I had gone but a short distance when I distinctly heard the neighing of horses and the sound of men moving . . . I had opportunely struck the head of the enemy's retreating column."

Johnson wheeled about and clattered back over the bridge, shouting orders for his column to deploy along the embankment below on both sides of the bridge, Steuart's brigade to the north, Nicholl's to the south. Skirmishers crossed the tracks into the woods. Andrews's artillery was close to the head of the column. Gunner J.W. Owens and his colleagues scrambled to move and unlimber the two cannons into position. He watched his pickets scramble back to the tracks as a long blue line advanced. Then Andrew's shouted out, "Load and fire at will!"

The Federals were in what one soldier called a "murderous trap." In the midst of a retreat, without artillery, they now had to fight their way across a bridge *and* form line of battle between the Pike and the woods. They had been literally blind-sided. There was chaos—but no panic. The Federals would make a fight of it. It centered at first on the bridge. Several charges failed to take the gun. The gunners loaded and fired at top speed, shortening fuses and then firing canister at point-blank range. The Federals could not cross, but instead dropped to the ground and began shooting down the gunners on the bridge. Andrews was badly wounded, and the original gun crew was all killed save one. A Confederate staff officer wrote:

> It was key to our position. Lt. C.S. Contee was in command. His men fell around him and all were killed and wounded but himself and one other . . . unsupported except for a line of bayonets in the railway cut . . . at every discharge the recoil carried the gun almost over the side of the bridge . . . two sets of cannoneers, 13 out of 15 men were killed or disabled."

Meanwhile, battle lines formed north and south at the bridge. The 110th and 122nd Ohio faced toward the woods and the guns of George Steuart's Confederate brigade that stood north of the bridge. South of the bridge the 123rd Ohio, the 18th Connecticut and the 67th Pennsylvania faced Francis Nicholls' men. The Federals were desperate, either to force the bridge or to hold the Pike open. They pushed the Confederate skirmishers out of the woods, but could get no closer to the railroad line.

Johnson worried most about his left (southern) flank, knowing that Milroy had three brigades in column. The third, McReynold's, might overlap his line near where the railroad crossed over a narrow lane. But it was at the rear of Milroy's column that conditions were at their chaotic worst. The shock of the collision at the head of the column sent tremors of fear to the non-combatant rear of the column. The 6th Maryland and the 67th Pennsylvania did briefly overlap the Confederate left, but the 2nd and 10th Louisiana regiments pulled out of line to refuse the flank. Closer to the bridge, the 13th Pennsylvania Cavalry tried to mount a charge, but the Confederate gunners on the ridge behind to the east saw them in time to turn their guns to the left, and open fire, stopping the charge before it could start.

At the center, a final effort to take the bridge failed. A soldier in the 18th Connecticut called the attack "fatal to the preservation of the 18th, but it saved General Milroy and his staff." The general had earlier boasted that the enemy might surround but would never capture him and he would prove right on both counts. Johnson himself rode after Milroy, following him northwest as far as the Opequon Creek. Milroy escaped when General Johnson's horse threw him into the creek. The Confederate general did capture other Yankees, waving them in with his "opera glass."

Nearly half of Milroy's men escaped, a tribute to the fight the column made along the Martinsburg Pike. The timing of Johnson's arrival at the bridge and the gallant stand by his artillerists determined the outcome. In all, the Confederates took 3,500 prisoners, eleven stands of colors and 175 horses.

Continue south down Milburn Road. This is the only Winchester Civil War site common to all three battles of Winchester. In 1862, Jackson rode down this lane as far as the bridge, where he halted his pursuit of Banks. In 1864, as we shall see, the great cavalry charge that climaxed the Third Battle began here. On your left, as you approach a T-intersection you will see the site of the Milburn Chapel and the Cemetery.

Milburn Cemetery

The Milburn Cemetery has graves from the 18th century. It is maintained by the Emmanuel United Methodist Church. Over the years David Fahnestock, a legendary Winchester auctioneer and a relative of Lt. Snowden Andrews, has mowed the grass. [John Fox]

Across from the cemetery see the ruins of the Easter house. Soldiers from the 67th Pennsylvania plundered the house during the battle, but it survived until 1960, when it burned.

Turn right onto McCann's Road [Rt. 838] at the house ruins and follow the lane past the gate and beneath the railroad to reach Martinsburg Pike [Rt. 11]. Just before you reach Rt. 11, you may want to retrace your steps to Milburn Road to walk into a truly unchanged past.

You'll see exactly what Union lieutenant colonel W.A. McKellip, 6th Maryland, saw in the first light of June 15, 1863. He described his regiment's advance off the Pike as they moved along the narrower road in "quick time and in perfect order . . . we moved, then, to a stone wall, that was running from the road, and facing toward the battery that was firing on us." The wall is still visible today on the north side of the lane. The colonel continued: "We moved to the railroad and halted, the battery in the meantime playing on us. From there we passed through the tunnel or arch, and down by a ravine that protected us from the enemy's battery."

As you move down the lane, you'll see the railroad overpass McKellip mentioned. Once you pass beneath the tracks, the grade is downhill and you can see clearly how the men were now protected from artillery fire from their left. McKellip recalled: "When we got to the house that stands on the left hand side . . . and when my regiment came up I posted myself at the gate and gave orders that none of my men should go inside, and none were allowed to go in." The house used to be visible on the northwest corner of the intersection but burned to the ground after a lightning strike several years ago. Today you can stand in front of the picket gate and imagine the soldiers filing past the house.

Lieutenant Colonel McKellip recalled: "The Colonel went to the head of the regiment and gave the command 'by the left flank, guide center!' We marched up the crest of that hill in line of battle. There we found the enemy in position, in line of battle, with artillery and too strong for us to cope with." The regiment pulled back into the intersection and then moved by the right flank, down the ravine to the right of the cemetery, still visible today, and so left the battle.

The Second Battle of Winchester had ended.

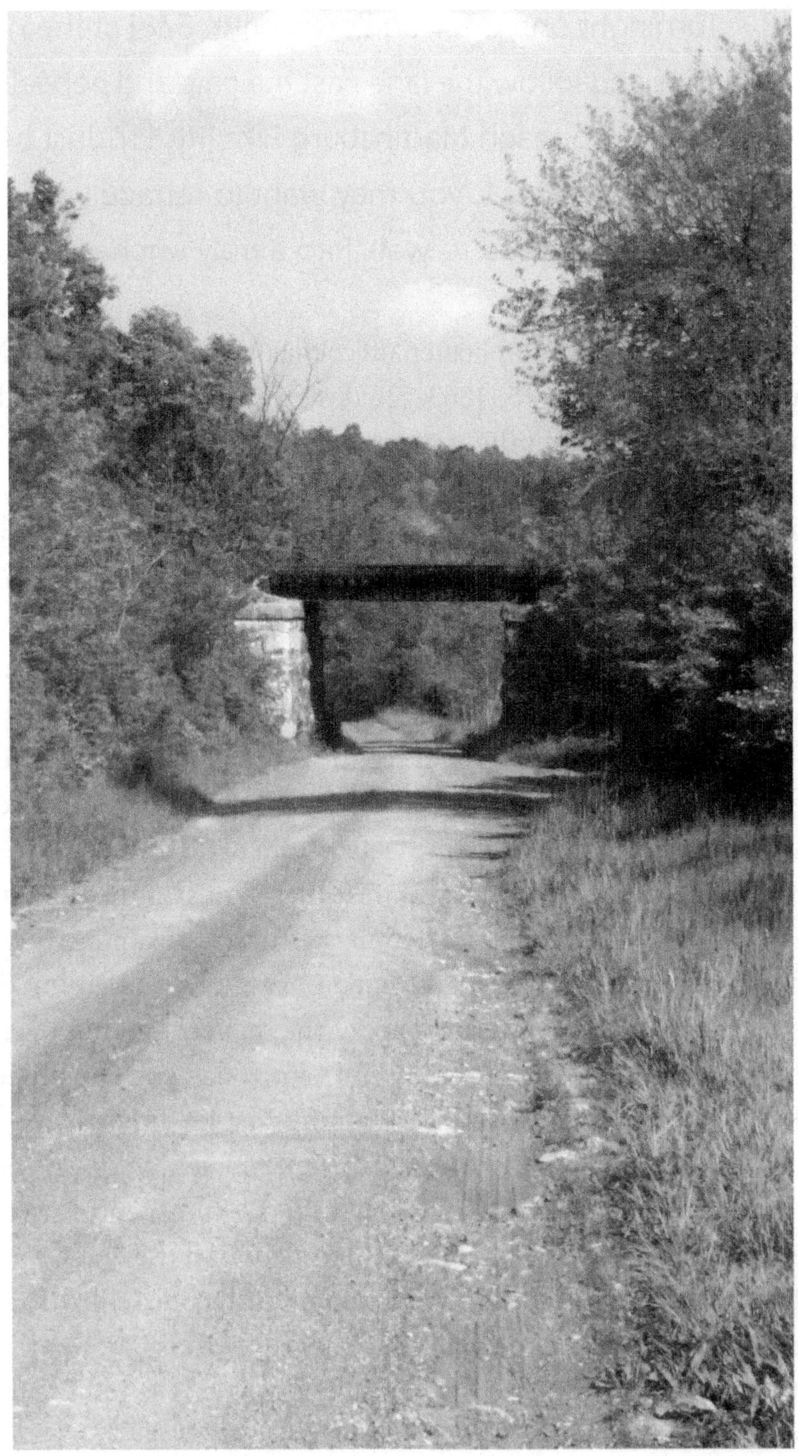

McCann Road and view of low ground to east that shielded 6th Maryland from Confederate view

[John Fox]

RETURN TO THE VISITORS CENTER

To reach the Visitors Center from Stephenson's Depot, take either McCann's Road or Old Charlestown Road back to Martinsburg Pike [Rt. 11]. Turn left. Cross under Interstate 81 bridge and turn left and drive south on Interstate 81 to exit 313A. Turn right onto Rt 50 West. At Millwood Avenue turn right. At South Pleasant Valley Avenue turn right and then turn right into Visitors Center which was your starting point.

Aftermath
Casualties
Second Battle of Winchester

Confederate	*Union*
47 killed	95 killed
218 wounded	373 wounded
3 missing or captured	3,975 missing or captured
Total Confederate Casualties 268	Total Union Casualties 4,443

The Confederates also captured 28 cannons: 23 at Winchester and 5 at Martinsburg. Mary Greenhow Lee commented that if Union general Nathaniel Banks had been the Confederate commissary in 1862, then Milroy was the new quartermaster.

Prior to sending their prisoners south, the Confederates marched them into Star Fort. Perhaps Confederate officers wanted the Union prisoners to take a last look at the foundation stones from Senator James Mason's destroyed house that Milroy had ordered brought to reinforce the walls of Star Fort.

The Union officers' wives, attired in their finest, presented a special problem. One Confederate remembered, "they started toward us, two by two, led by a greyclad soldier. All were in tears and excited our sympathy. 'What has become of Lieutenant or Captain or Colonel So and So?' Of course, we could give them no satisfactory answer."

In Winchester the following afternoon a group of ladies applauded generals Ewell and Early and asked them to speak a few words. Ewell was reported to have remarked, "I can't make a speech to ladies. I never made a speech but to *one* lady in my life. My friend General Early can speak." Early responded, "I never have been able to make a speech to *one* lady, much less to so many."

Mrs. Mary Lee noted in her diary that:

> Some of the girls have been busy for two days making a flag for "Fort Jackson" as General Ewell had christened the scene of the bombardment; it was to be raised this evening at 6 o'clock, but no one intended going from our house, not being willing to take the walk, but unexpectedly General Ewell sent his carriage, which holds five, for us . . . I declined going on the plea of being too old; they had a very pleasant time; it was a triumph to raise our flag over the 500 Yankee prisoners in the fort. When they returned, we had tea and the table looked so pretty.

When he learned of Ewell's victory, General Lee wrote to General James Longstreet, "Early's division stormed the enemy's works at Winchester, capturing their cannon, with little loss on our side. He is pushing on." Lee next sent word to President Davis: "God has again crowned the valor of our troops with success. Early's division stormed the enemy's enforcements at Winchester, capturing their artillery."

Federal authorities arrested General Milroy when he reached the safety of his own lines. He demanded a court of inquiry which met from August until late October, a short time after the Federal victory at Gettysburg. President Lincoln wisely concluded that "Serious blame is not necessarily due to any serious mistake and I cannot say that in this case that any of the officers are deserving of serious blame. No court martial is deemed necessary or proper . . ."

(The entire proceedings may be seen in the *Official Records of the War of Rebellion,* Vol. 27, part 2, pp 88–197.)

Afterword
Second Winchester & Gettysburg

In the aftermath of the defeat at Winchester, General Milroy later claimed that his "stand" at Winchester had crucially delayed the Confederate advance into Pennsylvania and had helped bring about the victory at the Battle of Gettysburg sixteen days later. Given the numerous variables and events that occurred between June 15 and July 1, his claim is difficult to substantiate.

Winchester did have a powerful effect on the Battle of Gettysburg, especially its first day, July 1. The fighting around Winchester was Ewell's first experience as a corps commander. The first day of Gettysburg was his second experience. In the late afternoon of July 1, the divisions led by Early and Rodes helped to drive the Federals from the fields north of Gettysburg, through town and onto the high ground south of town.

Ewell decided not to press an assault on Cemetery Hill, ground that Douglas Southall Freeman later described as "dangerous looking." Historians have explained Ewell's decision in a number of shopworn ways: he was not Jackson; he was not used to discretionary orders; or even that he was indecisive. Some have even suggested that Early might have influenced him against an attack.

I have always argued that Ewell wanted to fight at Gettysburg the same way he had fought at Winchester, sixteen days before. He decided not to press a frontal or headlong attack against an enemy on high ground, with excellent artillery support, late in the day. Perhaps, he believed that the next day might offer the opportunity to pry the Federals out of their positions with a wide flanking movement like the one he had successfully used at Winchester. The next day at Gettysburg, of course, offered no such opportunity.

Larry Maier's *Gateway to Gettysburg* [2002] is well-titled. Winchester was the Army of Northern Virginia's gateway to the Potomac crossings, and then to the Cumberland Valley, Chambersburg, Cashtown and McPherson's Ridge. Ewell's route took him to Carlisle, then south to Oak Ridge. The many variables now no longer mattered.

We read in Stephen Vincent Benet's *John Brown's Body,* Book 7:

> You say a fate rode a horse
>
> Ahead of those lumbering hosts, and in either hand

He carried a skein of omen. And when, at last,
He came to a certain umbrella-copse of trees
That never had heard a cannon or seen dead men,
He knotted the skeins together and flung them down
With a sound like metal . . .
Yet the riding fate,
Blind and deaf and a doom on a lunging horse,
Threw down his skeins and gathered the battle there.

Order of Battle at Second Winchester

June 14–15, 1863

Confederate
Second Corps, Army of Northern Virginia,

Lt. Gen. Richard S. Ewell

Major General Jubal A. Early's Division

Hays' Brigade—Brigadier General Harry T. Hays
- 5th Louisiana Infantry
- 6th Louisiana Infantry
- 7th Louisiana Infantry
- 8th Louisiana Infantry
- 9th Louisiana Infantry

Smith's Brigade—Brigadier General William Smith
- 31st Virginia Infantry
- 49th Virginia Infantry
- 52nd Virginia Infantry
- 58th Virginia Infantry

Hoke's Brigade—Colonel Isaac E. Avery
- 6th North Carolina Infantry
- 21st North Carolina Infantry
- 15th North Carolina Infantry
- 57th North Carolina Infantry

Gordon's Brigade—Brigadier General John B. Gordon
- 13th Georgia Infantry
- 26th Georgia Infantry
- 31st Georgia Infantry
- 38th Georgia Infantry
- 60th Georgia Infantry
- 61st Georgia Infantry

Artillery Battalion—Lt. Col. Hilary P. Jones
- Charlottesville Artillery
- Courtney Artillery
- Louisiana Guard Artillery
- Staunton Artillery

Brigadier General Edward Johnson's Division

Steuart's Brigade—Brigadier General George H. Steuart
- 1st Maryland Battalion Infantry
- 1st North Carolina Infantry
- 3rd North Carolina Infantry
- 10th Virginia Infantry
- 23rd Virginia Infantry
- 37th Virginia Infantry

Nicholls' Brigade—Colonel J.M. Williams
- 1st Louisiana Infantry
- 2nd Louisiana Infantry
- 10th Louisiana Infantry
- 14th Louisiana Infantry

Stonewall Brigade—Brigadier General James A. Walker

- 2nd Virginia Infantry
- 4th Virginia Infantry
- 5th Virginia Infantry
- 27th Virginia Infantry
- 33rd Virginia Infantry

Jones' Brigade—Brigadier General John M. Jones

- 21st Virginia Infantry
- 25th Virginia Infantry
- 42nd Virginia Infantry
- 44th Virginia Infantry
- 48th Virginia Infantry
- 50th Virginia Infantry

Artillery Battalion—Major J. W. Latimer

- 1st Maryland Battery
- Allegheny Artillery
- Chesapeake Artillery
- Lee Battery

Union
Second Division, VIII Corps
Major General Robert H. Milroy

First Brigade—Brigadier General Washington L. Elliott

- 110th Ohio Infantry
- 116th Ohio Infantry
- 122nd Ohio Infantry
- 123rd Ohio Infantry
- 12th Pennsylvania Cavalry
- Battery (L) 5th U.S. Artillery

Second Brigade—Colonel William G. Ely

- 18th Connecticut Infantry

87th Pennsylvania Infantry
5th Maryland
12th West Virginia
3rd West Virginia Cavalry
1st West Virginia Cavalry, Co. K
2nd West Virginia Cavalry, Cos. D & E
1st West Virginia Artillery, Battery D

Third Brigade—Colonel Andrew T. McReynolds
6th Maryland Infantry
1st New York Cavalry
67th Pennsylvania Infantry
Baltimore Battery, Maryland Light Artillery

Heavy Artillery—Captain William F. Martius
14th (1st) Massachusetts Heavy Artillery

CHAPTER 4

THE THIRD BATTLE OF WINCHESTER

SEPTEMBER 19, 1864

IN 1863 THE UNION WON the strategic initiative with victories at Vicksburg, Gettysburg, and Chattanooga. The following year the Union pressed its advantage, exerting sustained pressure everywhere on what remained of the Confederacy. The impending presidential election added urgency to strategy in both Washington and Richmond.

The spring of 1864 brought two campaigns to the Valley. Once again Winchester proved pivotal. The Third Battle of Winchester on September 19, 1864, ended Jubal Early's Valley Campaign and launched the fame of the new Union commander in the Valley, Phil H. Sheridan.

> Because the Forks of the Shenandoah River and the main stem Shenandoah River flow from south to north, military movement in the Valley from south to north is called "down" the Valley and movement from north to south is "up" the Valley. This is why the area around Winchester is known as the Lower Valley and the area southwest near Staunton is known as the Upper Valley. Failure to understand this will result in confusion.

When General Ulysses S. Grant took command of the Union armies at the beginning of 1864, he came east to Virginia to take virtual command of the Army of the Potomac. He planned to exert tremendous pressure on Lee's Army of Northern Virginia and also on the Valley. The Confederate victories over Union general Franz Sigel at New Market on May 15 was a setback, but on June 5, General David Hunter defeated a Confederate force at the Battle of Piedmont. Hunter then occupied Staunton and threatened Lynchburg. For Lee, the situation was as dire as in 1862 when three Union armies invaded the Valley. It seemed once again that the Valley might be lost. Lee wondered if he could repeat the diversionary strategy utilized by Stonewall Jackson in 1862 that had changed the course of the war. However, in 1862, Lee's adversary was the cautious McClellan who was always fearful of being outnumbered. In 1864, Grant had no such fear. Tactical defeats in the Wilderness seemed not to slow Grant. However, his bloody repulse at Cold Harbor in mid-June gave Lee an opportunity to revive the diversionary strategy of 1862.

Lee chose to send his Second Corps to the Valley to distract and divide Grant's Petersburg Campaign. However, the Second Corps, previously commanded by Jackson and Ewell, was a shell of its former self. It now numbered just over 8,000 men, less than half the number Ewell had led at Second Winchester the previous year. Nor was Ewell still in command. He had been replaced by Jubal Early. Early knew the Valley and Winchester well. He could be counted on to maintain the Corps' high standards of marching and fighting. Lee ordered Early to drive Hunter from the Valley and to "threaten the line of the Potomac," if possible, like Jackson had done in 1862. Early succeeded brilliantly.

General Jubal A. Early (1816–1894)

General Early led a division in the Second Battle of Winchester and commanded the Confederate force at the Third Battle of Winchester. [Library of Congress]

He drove Hunter from Lynchburg on June 17–18. He then came down the Valley and crossed the Potomac. He defeated General Lew Wallace at Monocacy, Maryland, on July 9, and skirmished with the defenders of Washington at Fort Stevens on July 11–12, before returning to Virginia. He next defeated General Horatio Wright at Cool Spring on July 18, and then beat General George Crook in the Second Battle of Kernstown on July 24. Confederate troops then recrossed the Potomac, and for the last time in the war, entered Maryland and Pennsylvania. General John McCausland's cavalry burned Chambersburg on July 30. By hard marching and fighting Early had won a series of battles on both sides of the Potomac, and diverted two Union army corps (VI and XIX) to the Valley.

These Confederate successes frustrated Lincoln and Grant. Early's victory at Kernstown led them to meet at Fort Monroe on July 31. They agreed that the Union command structure in the Valley needed to be simplified under the leadership of one aggressive commander. This new commander's assignment would be to seize the strategic initiative from Early and defeat him which would end the Valley's usefulness to the Confederacy. On August 1, Grant wrote to General Halleck in Washington: "I want [Major General Philip] Sheridan put in command of all the troops in the field, with instruction to get himself south of the enemy and follow him to the death."

Four days later Grant met with Sheridan at Monocacy Junction to give him command of the Middle Military Division and its striking force, the Army of the Shenandoah.

Sheridan was a professional soldier with a fine record compiled in the west. Grant brought him east in the spring and initially gave him command of the army's cavalry. His record was mixed—victory at Yellow Tavern (May 11), but defeat at Trevilian Station (June 12). Still, Grant liked Sheridan's aggressive nature. By September 14, Sheridan would command the Army of the Shenandoah with over 41,000 men in three infantry corps and a cavalry corps.

Major General Horatio Wright led the VI Corps which totaled 12,674 men in three divisions, led by David Russell, George Getty and James Ricketts. One of Russell's brigadiers, Emory Upton, had recently distinguished himself at Spotsylvania, in May, in the attack on the "Mule Shoe" salient.

General Philip H. Sheridan (1831–1888)

Commander of the Army of the Shenandoah in the Third Battle of Winchester, 1864. [Library of Congress]

The XIX Corps, under Major General William Emory, comprised two divisions led by William Dwight and Cuvier Grover. It had served most recently in Louisiana, and had just been brought east to Virginia.

The Army of West Virginia [sometimes referred as VIII Corps], a corps-sized unit, led by Major General George Crook, comprised two divisions. Crook's troops had formerly been known as the Army of the Kanawha. These were the Union troops most familiar with the Valley because they had fought at New Market, Piedmont and Lynchburg. When Sheridan came to the Valley he replaced Hunter with Crook. There were 7,140 men in its two divisions led by colonels Joseph

Thoburn and Isaac Duval. Two future American presidents, Colonel Rutherford B. Hayes and Captain William McKinley, both served under Crook.

Sheridan's force also included a cavalry corps commanded by Major General Alfred T. A. Torbert, which comprised three divisions of 9,000 horsemen. Torbert's men were better mounted and armed than the Confederate cavalry in the Valley and far more numerous. (Spencer repeating rifle shell casings are still found in abundance in the fields east and north of Winchester). Torbert's division commanders were Wesley Merritt, William Averell and James Wilson. A Confederate officer, General Bradley S. Johnson, gave Sheridan's troopers high marks: "... Sheridan's cavalry ... were about as good soldiers as ever took horse or drew saber." Because he was outnumbered and outgunned, Jubal Early had no margin for strategic error.

In 1862, Lee had been able to reinforce Jackson's command in the Valley. In 1864 he sought to do the same with Early's Second Corps. In early August, Lee dispatched General Richard Anderson with General Joseph Kershaw's division, Fitz Lee's cavalry and William Cutshaw's artillery battalion toward the Valley. The reinforcement made Sheridan cautious.

Lee's instruction to Anderson on August 11 sounded similar to 1862: "Any enterprise that can be taken to injure the enemy, obstruct or separate his forces ... embarrass his communication ... is desirable."

Sheridan's strength at this point was about 37,000 men, still a comfortable numerical superiority over the Confederates. However, he was unaware of the Confederate strength as he closely monitored Anderson's arrival to the Valley. Sheridan's men moved slowly from Harper's Ferry toward Berryville. After a sharp action at Guard Hill (Front Royal) on August 10, they pulled back to Halltown, which was located four miles west of Harper's Ferry. Early's troops followed.

From then until early September there followed a series of engagements that historian Scott Patchan describes as "quick hitting meeting engagements between forces engaged in reconnaissance." Sheridan learned that his cavalry could contend with Early's infantry. However, he did not yet know the diminutive size of Early's force while Early knew that his men were outnumbered. Early believed that he could bluff and deceive his opponent which would fulfill the objective of his campaign. The key was Anderson's force. With the siege of Petersburg underway near Richmond, how long could Anderson remain in the Valley? Would he be of more need to Lee than Early? On August 26, Lee wrote to Early: "I am in great need of his [Anderson's] troops, and if they can be spared from the Valley . . . I will order them back to Richmond. Let me know."

Early and Anderson agreed that some of Anderson's men could be spared. On September 14, Joseph Kershaw's division and Cutshaw's artillery headed east, leaving only Fitz Lee's cavalry as the Valley reinforcement. Early's force, though still dangerous, was now reduced to four divisions of infantry, two of cavalry and three battalions of artillery.

Major General John B. Gordon's division included the brigades of Clement N. Evans, William Terry and Zebulon York. Terry's brigade included the remnants of the Stonewall Brigade. Five of York's Louisiana regiments—the 4th, 6th, 7th, 8th and 9th—had fought in the First and Second Battles of Winchester.

Major General Stephen D. Ramseur's division was also made up of three brigades, led by John Pegram, Robert Johnson and Archibald Godwin. Johnson's brigade strength was sadly typical of the army in 1864—800 to 1,000 men in four regiments and a battalion of sharpshooters.

There were four brigades in Major General Robert E. Rodes' division. Cullen Battle now commanded Rodes' old brigade. Bryan Grimes, Phillip Cook and William Cox were the other brigadiers.

The fourth division, nominally Brigadier General Gabriel Wharton's was commanded by Major General John C. Breckinridge, the victor at New Market in May. Colonels Augustus Forsberg, Thomas Smith and George S. Patton, grandfather of the World War II general, commanded the brigades.

Fitzhugh Lee led the cavalry and commanded one division while Lunsford Lomax led the other division.

Colonel Thomas Carter was the artillery chief. There were three battalions, each led by Carter Braxton, Floyd King and William Nelson. Major James Breathed led a battalion of horse artillery.

Early's army numbered 18,000 men. Figures for September 10 showed 11,900 infantry, 5,606 cavalry, and 867 artillerists with 40 cannons.

In 1862, Lee had reinforced Jackson with Ewell's division, which gave Jackson the upper hand. In 1864 though, Lee was forced to recall Early's reinforcement, which gave the advantage to Sheridan and allowed him to go on the offensive. Sheridan learned this vital information from an unusual source—a Winchester

Unionist and Quaker school teacher named Rebecca Wright. One of Crook's officers was a friend of the Wright family. He told Sheridan of her willingness to send on any information she could glean about Early's army. At the same time, one of Sheridan's scouts enlisted the aid of the necessary "go-between" who was a free black man from nearby Millwood named Tom Laws. Laws had a Confederate pass into Winchester, where he sold produce. Laws brought Wright a note from Sheridan on September 16. Two days earlier she had learned from a talkative Confederate officer that Kershaw's troops had gone. After delivering her note, Laws waited most of the day for her to write a reply and return it to him. He then delivered her note with the important news to Sheridan. Union cavalry, patrolling east of Winchester confirmed Kershaw's departure. Sheridan reacted immediately. He planned to move his army south of Winchester on September 17, to cut Early off and isolate him in the lower Valley in the grasp of an overwhelming force. The Union timetable needed to be postponed when Sheridan learned that Grant wanted to see him in Charles Town.

Then Early made a move on the same day to divide his force. However, it would prove to be an error that he could not afford to make. He sent Gordon and Rodes' divisions to Martinsburg, to inflict more damage on the B&O. Breckinridge would stop at Stephenson. Ramseur, alone, remained east of Winchester. While in Martinsburg on September 18, Early learned of Grant's meeting with Sheridan the previous day. He sensed that he was now prey and he hurried south, but it would be too late. Averell's cavalry had informed Sheridan of Early's dispersal of his command. Sheridan prepared to strike at Winchester on September 19, while only Ramseur's division remained to guard the town.

The Berryville Pike became the main Union axis of advance over Opequon Creek at the Spout Spring Ford and then continued west through the gorge known as the Berryville Canyon. Once west of Berryville Canyon the ground opened up to the north and allowed the Union units to maneuver. Wilson's cavalry division led the way followed by three infantry corps. Averell's and Merritt's divisions, meanwhile, crossed the Opequon at several fords northeast of Winchester. Their mission was to slow and harass Early's infantry as it headed south from Martinsburg.

Sheridan's men crossed the Opequon at four different fords, from south to north: Spout Spring, Seiver's Ford, Rocky Ford and Locke's Ford. His plan was a simple one directed against a weaker and now dispersed enemy.

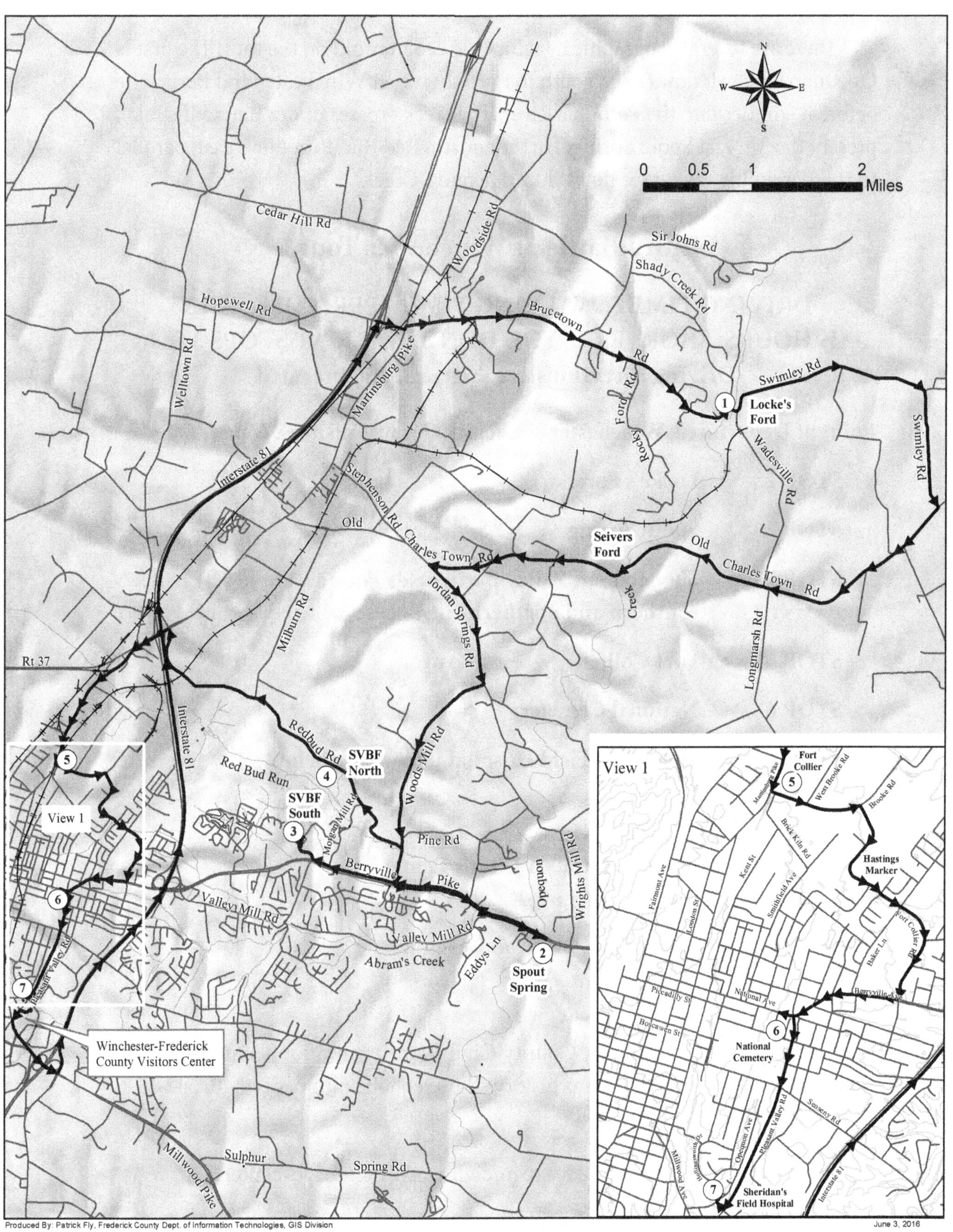

Third Battle of Winchester, September 19, 1864

There are several geographical factors to keep in mind on the tour. The first is Opequon Creek. It flows from south to north between Winchester and Berryville before it empties into the Potomac River. The creek crosses under Berryville Pike, present day Rt. 7, at Spout Spring. Farther north, Red Bud Run flows east, parallel to the Berryville Pike, as it flows into Opequon Creek.

Third Battle of Winchester Tour

DRIVING TIME & WALKING TIME APPROXIMATELY 4½ HOURS. SHORTER IF YOU DON'T WALK AT STOPS 3 & 4.

Driving directions are sans serif and indented

Point of Departure—Winchester-Frederick County Visitor's Center

STOP 1	**Locke's Ford**
STOP 2	**Spout Spring**
STOPS 3 & 4	**Shenandoah Valley Battlefields Foundation [SVBF] Site, southern and northern entrances**
STOP 5	**Fort Collier**
STOP 6	**National Cemetery**
STOP 7	**Sheridan's Field Hospital [Shawnee Spring]**

POINT OF DEPARTURE:

Winchester-Frederick County Visitor's Center

1400 S. Pleasant Valley Road

(Pleasant Valley Road and Millwood Avenue)

Open daily 9:00–5:00

The Winchester-Frederick County Civil War Orientation Center provides background for all local Civil War history. The telephone number is (540) 542-1326 or toll free (877) 871-1326

www.visitwinchesterva.com/civil-war-orientation-center

STOP 1 LOCKE'S FORD

To reach Locke's Ford, depart the Visitors Center and turn left onto Pleasant Valley Road. Turn left at the first stoplight which is Millwood Avenue. Go to the second light and turn left. Cross over I-81 and make left turn onto I-81 North. Drive three exits north to exit 321 [Clearbrook]. Turn right on Hopewell Road and go to light at intersection with Martinsburg Pike [Rt. 11]. Turn left onto Rt. 11 and turn right immediately onto Brucetown Road [Rt. 672]. Go several miles and pass through Brucetown. Bear sharply to right over narrow bridge that crosses Opequon Creek. Make an immediate left onto Swimley Road. After a short distance, at a sharp bend, you'll see a log house on the left. Locke's Ford is just behind the house, however this is private property so please respect that. Continue to follow Swimley Road [Rt. 672] for several miles until it dead ends at Old Charles Town Road [Rt. 761]. Turn right to head to Spout Spring, our next stop.

Locke's Ford

General George A. Custer's brigade fought its way across Opequon Creek against light opposition at this spot. [Bob Price]

Breckinridge's division guarded the lower fords of the Opequon early on the 19th with a small number of infantrymen from the 51st Virginia and some troopers from the 22nd Virginia Cavalry.

To cross the creek, Custer put two regiments on the high ground to lay down a covering fire for the 25th New York and then his Michigan regiments (1st, 5th, 6th and 7th) splashed across. When Colonel Thomas Devin's brigade went over at Rocky Ford, just upstream, they pushed the 30th Virginia Sharpshooters Battalion back toward Brucetown where there was some more infantry support plus two guns of Captain Thomas Bryan's battery. Confederate gunner Milton Wylie Humphries related what happened next: "The Federal cavalry charged up so close that I tried cutting or setting shrapnel fuses at zero . . . our cavalrymen who had lost their horses, thirty to forty, commenced firing . . . the enemy thought they were a line of infantry [and] wheeled about and retired."

For the rest of the morning the Federal cavalry skirmished with the Confederates as they neared Stephenson's Depot. The main Union thrust though was to the south at Spout Spring where much of Sheridan's infantry followed Wilson's cavalry division across the Opequon.

STOP 2 SPOUT SPRING

To reach Spout Spring, continue on Old Charles Town Road [Rt. 761]. Soon you will cross the Opequon, at Seiver's Ford. Go several miles until reaching the fork at Jordan Springs Market. Turn left onto Jordan Springs Road [Rt. 664]. At Woods Mill Road [Rt. 660] turn right. At Rt. 7 light [Berryville Pike] cross the median and turn left and enter the eastbound lane of Rt. 7. Drive 1.1 miles and make left U-turn at crossover [exercise Caution!] and pull onto side of westbound lane at pulloff. See Millbank House on hill to southwest. Directly to east is Rt. 7 bridge over Opequon Creek where Sheridan made his crossing at Spout Spring.

The Millbank House belonged to Daniel Wood, whose mill stood nearby. The Yankees burned the mill a few days before the battle. The house served as a field hospital during the battle. Later, the artist James L. Taylor sketched the house with hospital tents in the front.

The Antebellum Millbank House

On the south side of Rt. 7 just west of the Opequon Creek bridge at entrance to waste water treatment plant a driveway leads to the antebellum Millbank House (see p. 106). The house is not yet open to the public, but you can get a good view of the crossing site from the driveway. You may call the Fort Collier Civil War Center (540-323-0221) for permission.

If you don't want to go up the Millbank House driveway, you may want to take a look at the crossing site from this vantage point and then drive on to a better place to consider progress of Sheridan's army through the canyon. A good place to do that is at our next stop, the entrance to the Shenandoah Valley Battlefield Foundation's Third Battle of Winchester site.

Spout Spring looking east

This picture shows Spout Spring, the Berryville Pike-Opequon Creek crossing in 1901. The camera lens looks east toward Berryville and the direction that Wilson's cavalry came from when they crossed here before dawn on September 19, 1864, to enter the "Berryville Canyon" and begin the Third Battle of Winchester. Sheridan's infantry, the VI, XIX Corps and Army of West Virginia [VIII Corps] followed. [Walker Bond Family Papers, Stewart Bell, Jr. Archives Room, Handley Regional Library, Winchester, VA]

Spout Spring looking west

This image shows the Spout Spring crossing over Opequon Creek and Berryville Pike headed west toward the Berryville Canyon and Winchester. This photo was taken by Captain William Francis Tiemann, 159th New York, during a visit in 1888. He was a Union soldier captured during the Third Battle of Winchester. [Philip W. Tiemann Jr. Collection, Stewart Bell, Jr. Archives Room, Handley Regional Library, Winchester, VA]

When Wilson's cavalry came across just before dawn all signs seemed to point to a smooth and rapid execution of Sheridan's plan—getting through the Canyon before Early could reconcentrate his force to stop him.

And yet, as Helmuth von Moltke, then chief of the Prussian General Staff, wrote of his experience in the Prusso-Danish War a few months earlier: "no plan survives first contact with the enemy." And indeed, things went awry on the Berryville Pike. The gorge would have been a difficult trek for an army if it were unopposed. But Ramseur's infantry and Bradley Johnson's cavalry fought hard, giving ground only grudgingly. One of Wilson's troopers was heard to say of Ramseur's men: "They are gutty this morning. They mean to fight."

Millbank House today

This large Greek Revival house was owned by Daniel T. Wood during the war. It was used as a Union field hospital for several days beginning on September 19, 1864. It sits just west of the Opequon Creek crossing known as Spout Spring. [John Fox]

Wounded Union men began coming back, trailing blood. Makeshift hospitals sprang up on both sides of the road. As the cavalry moved on, and the first regiments of the VI Corps started through, soldiers could plainly see the surgeons at work. Although the Confederates could not stop this advance, they inflicted casualties and slowed Sheridan's men.

Then a new problem arose, a near disaster. Contrary to orders, Wright's VI Corps wagon trains came in behind the infantry, ahead of the XIX Corps, creating a "traffic jam" that slowed the advance still further.

Among the wounded who passed this way that morning was Captain Ira Gardner of the 14th Maine, a regiment in the XIX Corps. Surgeons amputated his arm in the yard at the home of Charles L. Wood. He returned to Winchester on September 19, 1901, and visited the Wood house. He saw his bloodstains on the floor of the room to which he had been carried, and he thanked Mrs. Wood again for her care. Mr. Wood had buried the arm in the yard, and then later moved it to the National Cemetery. The Captain long remembered the "night when my life hung in the balance with only a Confederate lady to nurse and care for me. May God bless this good lady."

Union captain John Williams DeForest wrote:

> The road was crowded with wagons, ambulances, gun carriages and caissons . . . on the right and on the left endless lines of infantry struggled through the underbrush . . . gravely watching us pass sat the hundreds of men who belong to an army but never fight . . . cooks, . . . servants, . . . skulkers . . . Here too were jammed squadrons of Wilson's cavalry . . . we met litters loaded with pallid sufferers, and passed a hospital tent where I saw surgeons bending over a table and beneath it amputated limbs lying in pools of blood.

Charles Wood House today

This was the place where Captain Ira Gardner was carried after being wounded in the arm. It is located on Red Bud Run east of the battlefield. [John Fox]

As officers and teamsters shouted and cursed, columns of infantry turned off the clogged track to stumble along the steep and narrow road shoulders. Persevering, the long line inched forward. Soon the first elements of the VI Corps were through, as the XIX Corps continued to slog forward.

The delay was Early's second reprieve. Resourceful, combative and determined, he made the most of it. A line of battle began to form. Ramseur's men fought on the Dinkle Farm just beyond the exit from the canyon, where the Pike, out in the open now veered southwestward to skirt the property.

Gordon's division moved up to a position just south of the Hackwood House and formed near Ramseur's left. Meanwhile, Rodes' men remained just to the north on the Martinsburg Pike. Rodes' troops soon hurried south to the sound of the guns and some of these Confederate veterans sensed that someone had erred, and their compatriots were fighting alone. The moment of truth was at hand. A Georgian wrote:

> I saw the infantry passing south up the Pike, some of them . . . weeping with fatigue . . . by this time the guns were roaring heavy near Winchester on the Berryville Road . . . the men began to see that something was wrong . . . couriers and staff officers were in a stir, riding at rapid gaits carrying orders . . . we privates knew that trouble was up.

Confederate artillery sat nearby in close support. Nelson's guns backed up Ramseur while Braxton's gunners stood farther north in support of Gordon. Meanwhile, Breathed's Horse Artillery sat north of Red Bud Run, ready to fire directly south into any Union attackers who crossed their front.

Once the VI and XIX Corps were clear of the canyon, Sheridan prepared for a general advance. It would not be easy. With the XIX Corps aligned north of the VI Corps, the Federals presented a very broad front. At the beginning of the advance the XIX Corps right was only 250 yards from Red Bud Run. The front widened, or opened up, as the advance continued. The terrain favored the Confederates. The VI Corps' lone avenue of advance, the Berryville Pike, became a particular problem. Some Union officers feared that movement along the Pike might drag the VI Corps away from the left of the XIX Corps as it moved straight ahead. The Federal advance began at 11:40 AM.

STOP 3 SHENANDOAH VALLEY BATTLEFIELDS FOUNDATION [SVBF] SITE, SOUTHERN ENTRANCE [APPROX. 90 MINUTE TO 2 HOUR WALK]

Shenandoah Valley Battlefields Foundation
(540) 740-4545
shenandoahatwar.org

To reach the site head west on Rt. 7 from Spout Spring about 1.7 miles and turn right at the traffic light onto First Woods Drive and go uphill toward Millbrook High School. (Keep in mind that the original roadbed through the Berryville Canyon is today's eastbound lane of Rt. 7, on your left, down the steep slope, on the floor of the gorge. It was, at best, a difficult and narrow passageway.) Make your first left before Millbrook High School and drive to stop sign. Turn right and go into parking lot behind school. You will see signs for the Third Winchester Battlefield.

There are two entrances to the site, the south entrance here behind Millbrook High School and another one farther north, which will be our next stop. From the south entrance we'll hike as far as the Hackwood Lane Wayside Marker—a walk of about 90 minutes to 2 hours depending on how long you linger at each marker. Going that far will take us through the early phases of the battle, and keep you within a reasonable distance of your vehicle.

One final note before you set out. From about 11:40 AM until sunset some 55,000 men fought here. The fighting was intense and bloody. Even eyewitnesses and participants sometimes disagreed about the location and sequence of some events. Positions changed during the course of the battle. For example, Confederate artillery positions early in the day were sometimes Union positions by mid-afternoon. But the wayside markers are clear and accurate. They give you the best possible on-site interpretation of this pivotal battle.

> Just inside the entrance you'll see directions for a trail marker for the "Union Rear." It marks the rear area of the XIX Corps at the time of its advance—11:40 AM. After viewing the marker retrace your steps and take the first trail on the right. It leads to a marker chronologically out of sequence with where we are now, but extremely important. This marker titled "Thoburn's Attack" is for Colonel Joseph Thoburn's division of the Army of West Virginia, marking its mid-afternoon advance west, paralleling Red Bud Run which flows by about 250 yards farther north.
>
> After reading "Thoburn's Attack" turn left and move to the next marker for "The First Woods—A Perfect Slaughterhouse." Then turn right and go to "The Middle Field, Bloodiest Ground of the Shenandoah Valley."

Be mindful of the themes underlying the terrible ebb and flow of the battle:

1. The Confederate defense, which was both aggressive and tenacious.

2. The great resiliency of Sheridan's army, which enabled it to overcome near disaster.

3. Sheridan's own ability to alter his plan as circumstances changed, to fight a battle far different from that planned.

> Also, note the marker to the right [north] that describes "Union Victories in the Valley" although a Union victory here was anything but certain at 11:40 AM on September 19.

The Confederates fought a defensive battle—without rifle pits or breastworks. But they did not wait for the Federals to close with them. Instead they launched counterattacks, aimed at gaps and perceived weak spots in the lines advancing toward them. The terrain made Union alignments difficult to maintain, creating dangerous gaps, vulnerable to counterattack.

Dinkle House [Pleasant Hill] that witnessed heavy fighting.

This image was taken about 1926. The house no longer stands and the farm has been turned into Gateway Plaza Shopping Center. [Jeff Chamberlin Collection, Stewart Bell, Jr. Archives Room, Handley Regional Library, Winchester, VA]

The most dangerous gap was caused by the Berryville Pike veering southwest to skirt the Dinkle property. It opened up vulnerable space between the right of the VI Corps, guiding on the Berryville Pike, and the left of the XIX Corps.

General John B. Gordon's division made the first counterattack, aimed at the XIX Corps' exposed left.

Major General John B. Gordon (1832–1904)

General John B. Gordon (1837–1904) survived five wounds in the Bloody Lane at Sharpsburg in 1862. He commanded a brigade in Early's division at the Second Battle of Winchester in 1863 and a division in Early's Valley Army in 1864. [Library of Congress]

Gordon's attack succeeded at first, but had no real chance of breaking the Union lines or "rolling it up." The weight of the Union advance blunted the attack. Regiments from Kiefer's brigade on the VI Corps' right forced the Confederates back in the direction of the Hackwood House.

Then, while Gordon rallied his men, Rodes' division came into line, now on Ramseur's left. This counterattack which Gordon was able to support, was far more powerful and dangerous. The marker for the Middle Field clearly describes and depicts this Confederate thrust because it gave Early his only chance to win an improbable victory to keep his campaign alive.

An officer in the 159th New York recalled the nightmare of the Middle Field:

> The regimental line was perfect, the men marching with precision and keeping well dressed on the colors. We were halted and kept up a steady fire . . . an aide dashed at full gallop across the field just in our rear who shouted "Retreat! Retreat!" Looking to our right we saw our force falling back . . . When we reached the ravine an order was given to rally which I at once repeated and tried to stop my men but before I could realize it we were surrounded by rebels one of whom aimed his musket at me demanded my sword which I had in my hand. I tendered it to him then he yelled "belt and all!" . . . so I unbuckled my belt and gave it to him with the best grace I could under the circumstances.

Union captain John Williams DeForest remembered a frightening scene:

> We were pitted against a regiment which was giving way. There were not more than 40 men left . . . my adjutant called me to look to the left . . . behold! Rickett's division was gone . . . in place of it there was a line of butternut . . . all I could do was retreat . . . we lost some prisoners as well as 115 men hit . . . the pike was crowded with fugitives . . . officers galloped about after skulkers, exhorting, commanding, threatening and swearing as officers do in such cases.

Grover's division lost more than 1,500 men here—killed, wounded, or captured.

As you leave the "Union Victories in the Valley" wayside follow the trail west toward the twin, facing rows of poplars at the far side of the field. These trees provide a canopy like tunnel over the old Hackwood Lane. We are moving now into Confederate lines, into the heart of the counterattack and defense.

Walking between the trees, after a short distance, you'll pass a sit-down rest area with benches installed by the local Boy Scouts of America chapter. Next you'll come to an intersecting path. Turn left, heading for the "Second Woods" wayside.

We have seen that General Cuvier Grover's division initially drove Gordon's attacking brigade back toward General Clement Evans' brigade. However, Union jubilation would not last long as Confederate general John Gordon rallied his command and was joined by Robert Rodes' men in a counterattack.

Follow the path from the "Second Woods" marker and at intersection turn right to the "Confederates Reform" marker.

We learn, as the marker notes that General Early stood close to the front and he clearly understood the gravity of the situation—"unless the force were driven back," he wrote, "the day was lost." Colonel Thomas Carter sat on horseback with General Early near Braxton's cannons as Union infantry closed in on the area. Braxton suggested "that the guns be double shotted with canister" and Carter agreed. Early believed their capture imminent and he soon raced away. However, Braxton's gun crews stood their position and never faltered. Carter recalled, "The guns fired as one when the front line of the enemy was almost close enough to feel the flash of the powder. For a moment the smoke hid all from view. When it cleared away we had the joy to see 'their banners rent and their columns riven,' and a field of flying, disorganized men scudding to the woods."

Follow the trail to the "West Woods" trail marker and note that the trail loops back to a point near the old Hackwood Lane

The Rodes-Gordon counterattack saved Early's army—for the moment—and threatened to wreck Sheridan's. Brigadier General Cullen A. Battle's all-Alabama brigade led the fight with Rodes' other brigades while brigades from Evans, Terry and York out of Gordon's division provided ferocious support. Captain Robert Parks of the 12th Alabama saw General Early nearby and remembered that "I raised my hat to the old man as we ran forward . . . we raised our well-known Rebel Yell and continued on . . ."

The Union army's commander tried to rally his men. Sheridan seemed to be everywhere at once, creating an almost electric and certainly inspiring moral force in a way that foreshadowed "Sheridan's Ride" exactly a month later, when he would rally his men at Cedar Creek. He simply refused to allow the contagion of defeat to spread, and he inspired the same determination in others. He had shown great foresight earlier in the day in holding General David Russell's VI Corps division back as a tactical reserve. Now Russell led his men into the gap. Emory Upton's brigade led the way. Upton soon fell wounded while Russell was killed.

A soldier in the 14th North Carolina aimed his rifle at an officer he believed was Russell. The Tar Heel described his target: "A brave man, he had on a new bright uniform, mounted on a beautiful charger. I told Colonel Bennett I was going to take a shot . . . the officer was in a thick woods and his horse had become entangled in vine. I aimed at his head and he fell from his horse."

General Rodes also fell dead. His biographer, Darrell Collins, believes that he died instantly from either a shell fragment or a bullet which hit him behind the ear. Long after the war, Cullen Battle remembered how he learned of his chief's death. Battle recalled Rodes' aide-de-camp, Major Peyton, riding up to tell him that Rodes had been killed and that Battle was now in command. However, a short time later, General Bryan Grimes appeared and insisted that he was in command. Battle deferred in good grace, but was very distressed to learn next that Early had halted the attack. (Battle may have intended his account to foreshadow what he saw as Early's similar decision at Cedar Creek, a month later).

A Confederate counterattack would probably have failed. Russell's division stood in the gap. Early's only reserve was Breckinridge's division at Stephenson. Sheridan still had an uncommitted infantry corps (Army of West Virginia) and two divisions of cavalry.

> Continue north and go past the trail intersection with old Hackwood Lane. Walk to the "Confederate Defense Setup" marker. Then continue farther north to the marker for the Hackwood House that is located just before trail drops down to cross Red Bud Run. This is our turnaround point for this section of the battlefield. Retrace your path to the old Hackwood Lane [and the tree canopy] where you will turn left. Once you exit the tree canopy bear right or left and continue back to the parking lot.

The Confederate Defense marker is for Lieutenant Colonel Carter Braxton's seven gun battery which was parked wheel hub to wheel hub. Artillery support was crucial for Early's outnumbered infantry because without Braxton's guns, Early might have been driven from the field hours earlier. Braxton's Battery, supported by Breathed's Horse Artillery firing across Red Bud Run, shattered the Union advance. Colonel Thomas Carter concurred with this assessment as he wrote post-war: "At the Battle of Winchester Early's army would have been whipped before noon but for the artillery."

After the restoration of the Union line, Early might have chosen to withdraw in good order. But it was not in his combative nature to do so and Sheridan would probably not have allowed him to pull away.

Indeed, some of the bloodiest fighting of the day took place in the interval between the restoration of the line and Sheridan's next attack against the Confederate left. During this brief interlude, Captain DeForest wrote:

> Both sides were lying low . . . the only signs of battle were long stretches of smoke from musketry and graceful, rolling masses of smoke from

> the batteries . . . our adversaries were no doubt good shots and besides they fired more continuously than we did . . . they fought more like redskins, or hunters, than we . . . they lost fewer men, though they were far inferior in numbers.

All of the descriptions, Union and Confederate, point to this standoff at midday as the bloodiest place of the battle. According to Elisha Hunt Rodes, "The rebels seemed to have the exact range of our line."

Confederate Horace Smith wrote:

> The old boys say they never heard heavier musketry . . . a twelve-pound shell came and went under one of the gunners . . . taking off two large pieces of his rear and pushing out bone . . . he is a horrid object . . . shells took off Averitt's leg.

Captain Albert Artmen of the 14th Pennsylvania Cavalry wrote, "At every breath scores of men fell out of the ranks dead or wounded." According to Harris Beecher, of the 114th New York, "Blood was on everything—everywhere—was splattered upon bushes—was gathered in ghastly puddles upon the ground." Another soldier wrote, "It was lay on our back, load, get up, aim, fire—on my right three men were shot . . . on my left two were laid low . . . I loaded and fired about one hundred rounds."

Captain DeForest recalled "the men on both sides were nearly all old soldiers who knew their deadly business . . . a man was hit every few seconds." The 8th Vermont's sergeant Kirk Brown wrote, "The veterans of Stonewall Jackson fired amazingly low . . . their bullets caught the hiding places of the men with fatal accuracy.

Hackwood would be the focal point of Sheridan's next attack, made by the two divisions of the Army of West Virginia [VIII Corps]. Later, he and General George Crook would quarrel bitterly over whose plan it had been. In any event, Thoburn's division was to advance west along Red Bud Run's south bank. Duval's division was to retrace its steps through the canyon as far as a short and narrow road leading across Red Bud Run to its north bank. Duval then would move west, re-cross the run and attack in support of Thoburn.

STOP 4 SHENANDOAH VALLEY BATTLEFIELDS FOUNDATION [SVBF] THIRD WINCHESTER SITE, NORTH ENTRANCE [APPROX. 45 MINUTE WALK]

To reach Stop 4, the northern entrance to the SVBF site, to follow Duval's attack, return to Rt. 7 and turn left heading east, in the left lane. Drive ½ mile and take left exit onto Woods Mill Road [Rt. 660]. Make the 2nd left onto Redbud Road [Rt. 661] and drive 2.3 miles. Turn left into the SVBF lot which is not well marked. Across the street from the parking lot is the Shenandoah Valley Battlefields Foundation Third Winchester Orientation Center which is worth a stop if it is open.

Note the SVBF marker in the parking area, "A Gallery of Future Leaders." It describes the post-war accomplishments of thirteen Union and Confederate officers who fought here. Besides Early and Sheridan, these include two future presidents, Rutherford B. Hayes and William S. McKinley.

The walking trail that begins here will take about 45 minutes and leads you to the steep bluffs overlooking Red Bud Run, then down the slope and over the sturdy bridge. The bridge site ahead of us is one of the most rewarding Civil War experiences the Valley has to offer.

At about 2:30 Colonel Isaac Duval's Union men began their advance to Red Bud Run from this point.

The trail leads first to the marker for Captain Breathed's "Confederate Horse Artillery" position from earlier in the day. Confederate units on the north bank have pulled out by this time, and the field is now a Union artillery position. The next wayside is for "Crook's Attack" followed by a descent down to a marker for "Red Bud Run." This is the point to retrace your path back to the parking lot. If you continued across Red Bud Run and uphill you would come to the marker for the "Hackwood House" that you previously saw from the south entrance hike.

Duval was wounded before his men reached the near bank. Colonel Rutherford B. Hayes of the 23rd Ohio took command. The division crossed at various points, this being the most difficult. Conditions were at their worst here. The creek here was a swampy morass, or slough, between the steep banks you see. But as Hayes wrote:

> To stop was death. To go on was probably the same, but on we started again. My horse plunged in and mired down. I jumped off and on all fours succeeded in reaching the rebel side, but alone—hundreds were struggling in the stream.

Hayes' men followed him across and the division gained a foothold on the south bank. Soon the fighting spilled over onto the grounds of Hackwood, the large estate just upstream. Here the fighting became even more ferocious and lethal. Captain Russell Hastings of the 23rd Ohio marveled, "What stubborn fellows Gordon and his men were. Why could not our sharpshooters bring down those officers riding backward and forward in the rear of Gordon's line?"

Colonel William Lincoln, of the 34th Massachusetts wrote, "Half the regiment went down . . . every man, living or dead, was already buried in the grass which the enemy's musketry was mowing close and clean."

Once clear of the creek, the Federals passed over the Hackwood Farm and the open fields beyond, where Captain Hastings fell wounded. Here, in the open, the men were exposed to Confederate artillery. Again, modern-day ground evidence clearly shows that Early's artillery, firing from beyond Hackwood and from Fort Collier, held off the Federals, saving his flank for a few more hours.

Modern Hackwood House from north

Hackwood has been extensively restored since it was first built in 1777. The house lay in the path of Crook's infantry in the Third Battle. The house is easily visible from the northbound lanes of Interstate 81, between exits for Route 7 and Stephenson. [WFCHS, Stewart Bell, Jr. Archives Room, Handley Regional Library, Winchester, VA]

War-era Hackwood House

View of Hackwood from the south. Writing on back of image indicates troops on porch are Confederate but on closer inspection they appear to be Federal troops. [Julius and Faye Armel]

The concerted attack by two divisions from the Army of West Virginia [VIII Corps] had sliced across Red Bud Run and driven Gordon's division away from what had been the position anchoring Early's left. Still Early gave no thought to withdrawal. His flank had been turned, but his line had not been "rolled up." The Confederates withdrew closer to Winchester and formed a contracted L-shaped line. The left flanks now stretched from Star Fort to Fort Collier to a spot known as the Smithfield Redoubt. Sheridan continued to urge a relentless attack against Early's new left flank.

Major General Wesley Merritt (1834–1910)

Merritt commanded one of Sheridan's three cavalry divisions at Winchester. He wrote of the charge on Fort Collier, "It was a noble work well done—a theme for the poet; a scene for the painter." [Library of Congress]

"The Final Charge at Winchester" by Thure de Thulstrup

Fort Collier has yet to find its poet, but its painter is Thure de Thulstrup (1848–1930).

STOP 5 FORT COLLIER

To reach Stop 5, Fort Collier, turn left from parking lot onto Redbud Road. At the light turn left on Rt. 11. Pass under I-81 and drive straight in left lane. Bear left at sign that says "Winchester Business Rt. 11 South." Cross railroad tracks and turn left at light onto Brooke Road. Make an immediate left onto a gravel road into the entrance for the Fort Collier Civil War Center. A Virginia Civil War Trails marker greets you at the entrance, with the Stine House looming behind.

Together with the SVBF site, Fort Collier today represents a great victory for historic preservation. The Fort Collier Civil War Center (540-323-0221) gathered funds and fought hard to save the site from demolition and/or "development" to transform it into a great interpretive asset for the Third Battle.

The Trails marker at the entrance recalls General Wesley Merritt's description of the great cavalry charge that swept over and around the fort as "a scene for a painter." The site found its painter in Thure de Thulstrup's "Last Charge at Winchester" depicted on

Ft. Collier earthworks

Earthworks on the north side of the fort that saw the brunt of the Union cavalry charge. [Bob Price]

the marker. Other markers at the site describe the construction of the fort in 1862, the nature of Civil War earthworks in general, the Stine House at its center (the original house did not survive the battle), the course of the battle down to its climax, and the charge itself.

Stine House at Ft. Collier

The Stine House was built around 1866, replacing the house destroyed in the battle. The Stine family cemetery was just to the right of the picture above. Today the house remains largely surrounded by the Confederate earthworks built in 1861. On September 19, 1864, the fort's defenders were far too few to repel the largest cavalry charge of the Civil War. [Bob Price]

Harriett Griffith, a young Winchester girl, visited the Stine House in 1861 and witnessed the construction of Fort Collier around it.

Harriett Griffith described her August 21, 1861, visit to Fort Collier. "I have this day visited the breastworks or fortifications out on the Martinsburg Pike with Father and Johnnie. Was exceedingly interested. First work of the kind I'd ever seen. The first time I was ever so near a cannon. I looked into them. The cannon balls weigh 42 pounds each. There were four cannons planted and much ammunition there. A great many men were working, saw the magazines. They have several rifle ports which seem so secure. I have read of them, but have never seen them. They had several masked batteries. It seems so real strong and well built. There is a high embankment of sand bags, barrels, and brush covered with dirt, part sodded over. They intend to sod it with a big ditch on the lower side. They have completely surrounded Stine's House which is now occupied by soldiers some of whom were working there, some cooking, some washing, some on guard, and some lounging, and some sleeping . . . Surely it is something to be remembered but I hope it will never be used."

Fort Collier was a strong position but had few Confederate defenders on the afternoon of September 19. The force comprised some of Fitzhugh Lee's cavalrymen (he had been wounded and left the field), some of Breckenridge's infantry and two or three guns of Captain George Chapman's Monroe Artillery.

Artillerist Milton Wylie Humphreys from the battery wrote:

> Our army was now two sides of a rectangle with the infantry scattered within the angle . . . there was nothing but infantry and very little artillery pieces across the Martinsburg Road . . . our lines formed a gentle curve around the east and north of Winchester a few hundred yards from the town . . . September days run long in Winchester; by 5:00 there was more than ample light for the unleashing of one more blow, one more trial yet to be endured . . . Everything seemed deadly quiet.

The great Union cavalry charge, of about 6,000 troopers represented the largest charge during the Civil War. Its aim was to crush the entire left flank of Jubal Early's Army of the Valley.

Averill's division began the advance south from Stephenson, Colonel James Schoonmaker's brigade on the west side of the pike, Powell's on the east. Custer, Devin, and then Lowell's brigades, of Merritt's division rode across the 1863 battlefield, joining Averill's brigades, all now bearing down on Rutherford's farm (now the shopping center, "Rutherford's Crossing"). Four brigades abreast (Schoonmaker, Powell, Custer and Devin) they made short work of an attempted Confederate delaying action. Two of Devin's regiments—the 1st New York Dragoons and the 9th New York, caught Colonel Patton's retreating brigade out in the open. Henry Kyd Douglas described the result:

> For the first time I saw a division [sic] of infantry, or what was left of one, form a hollow square to repel cavalry.

Devin recalled how . . . "they dashed on the unfortunate infantry who were vainly endeavoring to form."

Moving fast now, the thundering wave of horsemen began to ride over and around the disintegrating Confederate defenses. Schoonmaker led a dismounted charge that overran and took Star Fort. A desperate Jubal Early ordered Munford's cavalry to ride from Senseny Road to his dissolving left. Two guns from Captain John Schoemaker's Battery kept up a brave fire from the redoubt on today's Smithfield Avenue, but Early's left was doomed, and the battle now lost.

The charge on Fort Collier was unforgettable to anyone who saw it. Wesley Merritt described it as "a theme for the poet, a scene for the painter." He also recalled that, "Custer led it boot to boot. The enemy's line broke into a thousand fragments under the attack." A Vermont soldier wrote, " 'Boys, look at that!' We did and saw a sight to be remembered a lifetime. In solid columns with drawn sabers flashing in the sun and without firing a shot came a brigade of troopers like a thunderclap out of a clear sky and that bolt struck home."

A Confederate witness described the great charge, "I never saw such a sight in my life as that of the tremendous force, the flying banners, sparking bayonets and flashing sabers moving from the north and east upon the left flank of our army."

A deep ditch ringed the earthworks. It is doubtful if any of the horsemen could have leapt the ditch and then climbed up the steep parapet. Most likely the attack swirled around the fort and found its entrance, in the works facing town.

Some cavalrymen may have dismounted and gone on without their horses or led them in and remounted.

Henry P. Morrison, 4th Virginia Infantry, wrote to his brother the following day:

> The Yankee cavalry were all mixed up with us and were in many instances knocked off their horses by the butt end of muskets . . . having no gun I gathered a club . . . I saw Yankees shot by men whom they had halted . . . We lost heavily. Out of the sixteen officers this battalion has only four left.

Once the Union cavalry was within the works, Merritt watched some Confederates surrender while "others hung tenaciously to their muskets, using them with their muzzles against our soldiers' breasts, and a number took refuge in a house and fought through the doors and windows, but the day was won . . . It was a noble work well done."

The riders swept over everything in their path, like blue waves breaching over and around sand castles. There were too many horsemen coming too fast for the few remaining defenders to have any chance. But even in their last extremity the gun crews stayed at their pieces, firing until the cannons were empty, or, in Milton Humphreys' case, the gun was so fouled that charges couldn't be rammed home. Humphreys' crew somehow moved their gun out of Fort Collier. They rode south toward town and stopped on the now crowded Berryville Pike to try to ram free the gun's choked barrel. General Early saw them there. Fearing for their lives, he ordered them to stop and get to safety, but one of the men, who probably failed to recognize the army commander replied ungraciously, "Go to hell you damned old clodhopper and tend to your own business."

Dudley Vaill, of the 2nd Connecticut Volunteer Infantry (The County Regiment) remembered what he saw in the fort: ". . . their abandoned artillery (2 pieces) which had done so much damage . . . hissing hot with action, with their miserable rac-a-bone a horses attached."

At the moment the Union charge struck home, Sheridan sprang into action, ordering an assault all along the line. Ohio captain Russell Hastings remembered that Sheridan "rode down to us and told us to push on . . . all caught the enthusiasm he displayed." Lieutenant Colonel Gordon Clark of the 119th Pennsylvania wrote that the army commander "rode along amidst the cheer of the whole line . . . the enthusiasm of the men became unbounded."

For Confederate captain Robert Parks it was the darkest day of the war as he wrote, "The men became impressed with the terrible, unendurable idea that they were flanked and began to retreat in confusion. It was a sad, humiliating sight, but such a handful of worn out men could not successfully withstand such overwhelming odds."

Captain Robert Funkhouser of the 49th Virginia Regiment, fighting with Ramseur's division on the Berryville Pike, had been wounded in the head. He recalled being helped to town, first on the arms of two soldiers and then in a military ambulance that left him on a Winchester street. With Yankee cavalry charging close, an old black man slowed another passing wagon and pulled him up onto the floorboards. Dropped off again south of town, Funkhouser noted, "I sat down on the roadside very giddy and weak . . . bloody down to my shoes."

Early, who had come so close to victory, was composed and resourceful in defeat. He quickly ordered a detachment of cavalry and artillery under Colonel Thomas Munford to drive the Yankees out of Star Fort just north of town. Munford succeeded, and then he opened a covering fire for Early's retreat. Early organized a line of last resistance, a last stand, that stretched from the intersection of today's Cork Street and Pleasant Valley Road into the grounds of the present National Cemetery. The remains of Confederate earthworks are still visible along Pleasant Valley Road just beyond the Cork Street intersection.

STOP 6 NATIONAL CEMETERY

To reach Stop 6, the National Cemetery, turn left out of Fort Collier onto Brooke Road. Follow it to Fort Collier Road and turn right.

After you pass the Frederick County Detention Facility on the left, look on the left for a wrought-iron fence around a small marker stone. The stone marks the spot where (then) Captain Russell Hastings of the 23rd Ohio was wounded, losing his leg. A local historian and author, Allan Tischler, installed the fence many years ago.

Continue on Fort Collier Road until you reach Berryville Avenue and turn right. Drive 7/10 mile and see the Winchester National Cemetery on the left. You can pull into the cemetery's very small parking area or park on the street.

Monument to Captain Russell Hastings, 23rd Ohio

This is the spot where Hastings was wounded and lost a leg. It is one of only two Winchester battlefield monuments outside of local cemeteries. [John Fox]

The National Cemetery, dedicated in 1868, contains the graves of 4,491 Union soldiers killed in fighting around Winchester throughout the war. Of these, 2,110 are known while 2,381 are unknown. The cemetery also contains notable monuments. To the right of the entrance, the historical marker describes the final Confederate position in the Third Battle of Winchester. Between the entrance and the flagpole at the center of the cemetery are monuments to the 114th New York Volunteer Infantry, the soldiers of New Hampshire, the men of the 123rd Ohio Volunteer Infantry, and the soldiers of Pennsylvania. Just beyond and to the left of the flagpole is the memorial to the VI Corps. Beyond, in the corner of the cemetery, are two monuments to the 8th Vermont Regiment, one commemorating its bayonet charge in the Third Battle of Winchester. It is "committed to the care

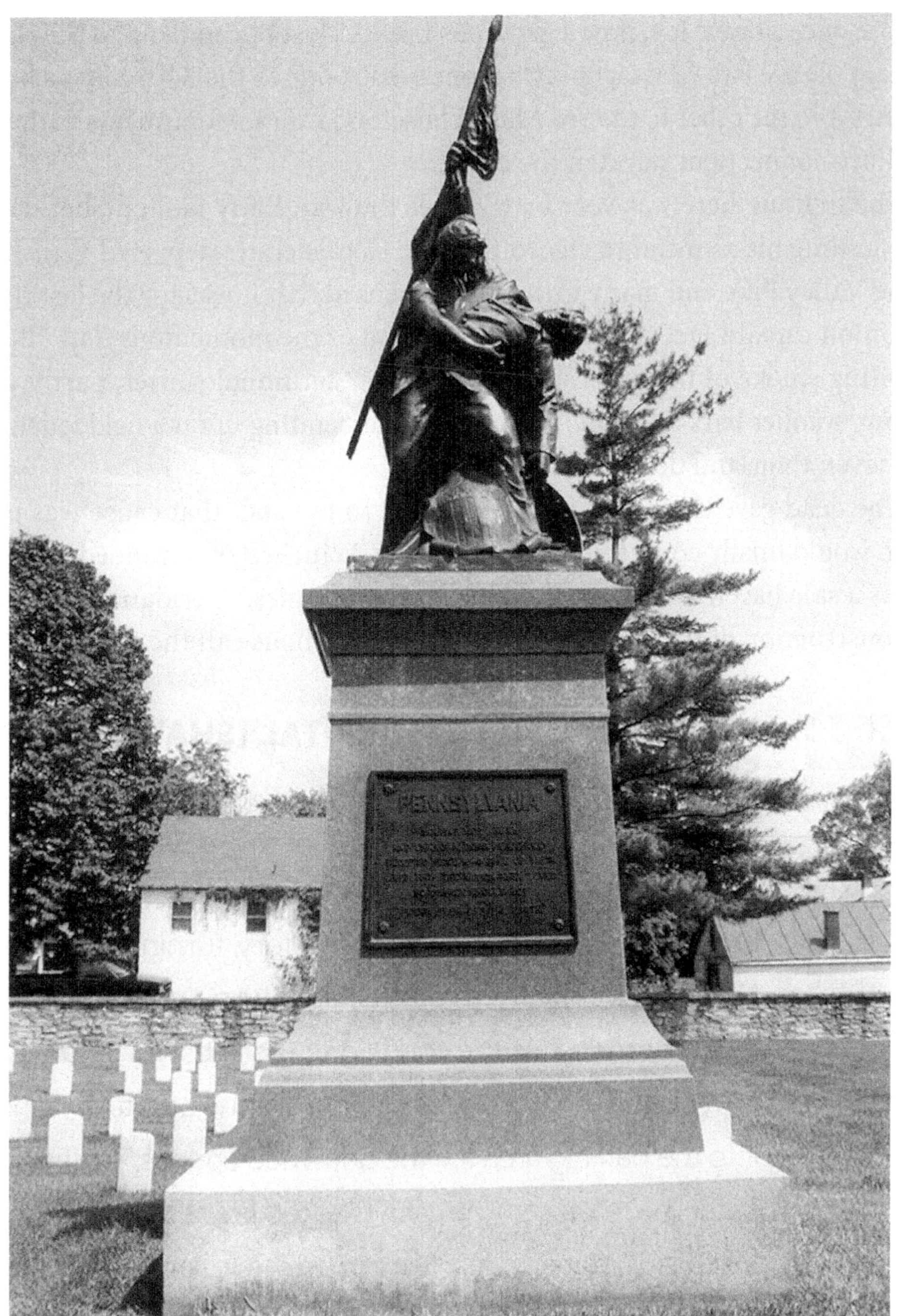

Pennsylvania Cemetery Monument in Winchester National Cemetery

When the Confederate line of battle gave way, some regiments rallied briefly on the high ground in today's National Cemetery before retreating south. Note that the Stonewall Confederate Cemetery is directly across the street from the rear wall of the National Cemetery. [Bob Price]

of those once a brave foe, now a generous friend." Just beyond and to the right of the flagpole are two Massachusetts monuments, one to the 34th Massachusetts Infantry and the other to the 3rd Massachusetts Cavalry. Monuments to the 12th and 18th Connecticut stand in the corner.

The fighting here was very brief. After the war, Early faulted Sheridan for not pursuing his army more vigorously. The Confederates departed Winchester on the Valley Pike and many townspeople sensed that it was for the last time.

Union captain DeForest described the end of the momentous day: "Behind the piling smoke of the guns spread a crimson autumnal sunset, partly veiled by long, somber bars of cloud . . . night was descending upon a field laden with near seven thousand dead and wounded."

The dead gave their lives for their cause. In the end, that cause was peace, which would finally come the following spring. Winchester continued its reputation as a safe haven for the wounded from both armies. Sheridan soon ordered the construction of the Sheridan Field Hospital to house all the invalids.

STOP 7 SHERIDAN'S FIELD HOSPITAL [SHAWNEE SPRING]

The spot of this large field hospital will be our last stop. To reach the Shawnee Springs Preserve, site of the hospital, leave the National Cemetery, turning right on National Avenue. At the traffic light turn right on South Pleasant Valley. At the third light, Hollingsworth Drive, turn right. Turn left on Opequon Avenue and turn right into the parking area for the Shawnee Springs Preserve. Later, to return to the Winchester-Frederick County Visitors Center turn left out of parking lot and then take first right. At light turn right onto Pleasant Valley Avenue and take next left into the Visitors Center.

The Sheridan Field Hospital was the largest of its kind in the war and the largest in American history until World War I.

On our tour we saw the locations of two makeshift hospitals, at the Daniel Wood house [Millbank] and the Charles Wood house. Similar sites sprang up in many places during the battle, some in Winchester homes. Another was at the Taylor Hotel located in downtown Winchester at 119-121 N. Loudoun Street.

The 10th Vermont's lieutenant Lemuel Abijah Abbott, who was himself wounded, claimed that 1,300 men were crammed into the Taylor Hotel. The number is probably an exaggeration, but his description of the look of the place rings true, similar to most descriptions of makeshift hospitals. He recorded, "I have seen piles of arms and legs today at the hospital thrown from the windows, as big as haystacks."

It should be noted in passing that amputation was one of the few lifesaving measures available to Civil War surgeons. But the larger point is that the Sheridan Field Hospital significantly raised the standard of care.

Several days after the battle ended, Union surgeon John H. Brinton arrived in Winchester. Brinton closed the many hospitals scattered through the area and he ordered that all the wounded be brought to Shawnee Springs, along Town Run, on the eastern edge of Winchester. As tents and more surgeons came in from Harpers Ferry, a vast tent city began to take shape by the end of the month. Soon more than 3,500 wounded men received shelter in 400 tents that were heated with the California Heating System. This new system used brick-lined fire pits, heated iron spikes and chimneys. The tents stood on platforms, and the heat rose up through the floorboards. Earth excavated for the channels, or ducts, was used to seal the bottom edges of the tents. Traces of this heating system can still be seen at the site.

In all, some 14,500 soldiers who were wounded at Third Winchester, Fisher's Hill (September 21–22), and Cedar Creek (October 19) received treatment at this facility. Soldiers who recovered enough to be moved left this field hospital via a limestone road, still visible in the woods, which led to the Valley Pike, and onward to Harpers Ferry.

At Sheridan's initiative, the Union command did all that was possible to care for the wounded, surely saving many lives. But even at its best, Civil War medicine lacked sterilization and adequate sanitation.

One of the thousands of Union soldiers who received treatment here was Corporal Anson Shuey of the 93rd Pennsylvania. A friend and teamster named Haske wrote Shuey's wife a heartbreaking letter that he composed over several days.

> He is well taken care of. He is in the care of Dr. W.A. Berry of Jonetown(sic). He spoke in favorable terms of the recovery of your Husband, although he is weak caused by the loss of blood. I am indeed sorry that your Husband befell with such a horrible wound.
>
> Supplyes are hard to get here. They must be brought from Harpers Ferry a distance of 32 miles. So No Daut he will be sent North as soon as convenient.
>
> My time is out on the 7th of Next Month.
>
> A wounded soldier's friend. S.S. Haske. For Your husband, Anson B. Shuey, your Husband died this morning at 6 o'clock the morning, Sept. 28th, 1864.

Aftermath
Casualties
Third Battle of Winchester

Confederate	*Union*
220 killed	697 killed
1,567 wounded	3,983 wounded
1,818 missing or captured	338 missing or captured
Total Confederate Casualties 3,605	Total Union Casualties 5,018

Word of Early's defeat soon reached Lee at Petersburg and he passed the sad information on to President Davis: ". . . the enemy advanced on Winchester . . . his attack was resisted from early in the day to near night when [Early] was compelled to retire. Our loss is reported as severe."

Belatedly, Lee returned Joseph Kershaw's division as reinforcements to Early, but the battle had ended. Early had lost the initiative, and could not regain the upper hand despite two more Valley battles that would be fought over the following month.

From Washington, President Lincoln sent this congratulatory note to Sheridan: "Have just heard of your great victory. God bless you all, officers and men. Strongly inclined to come up and see you."

But Lincoln never came. Three more Union victories followed in quick succession at Fisher's Hill, Tom's Brook and Cedar Creek. The Valley's last wartime harvest went up in smoke at the end of September as Union cavalry torched farmhouses, barns and mills during the Great Burning. Winchester would not change hands again as its long war was over.

Order of Battle at Third Winchester

September 19, 1864

Union
Army of the Shenandoah
Major General Philip H. Sheridan

VI Corps—Major General Horatio G. Wright

First Division—Brigadier General David Russell (KIA); Brigadier General Emory Upton (WIA); Colonel Oliver Edwards

First Brigade Colonel William Penrose
- 4th New Jersey
- 10th New Jersey
- 15th New Jersey

Second Brigade Brigadier General Emory Upton; Colonel Joseph Hamblin
- 2nd Connecticut Heavy Artillery (as infantry)
- 65th New York
- 121st New York
- 95th Pennsylvania Battalion
- 96th Pennsylvania Battalion

Third Brigade Colonel Oliver Edwards

- 37th Massachusetts
- 49th Pennsylvania
- 82nd Pennsylvania
- 119th Pennsylvania
- 2nd Rhode Island Battalion
- 5th Wisconsin Battalion

Second Division—Brigadier General George W. Getty

First Brigade Brigadier General Lewis A. Grant

- 2nd Vermont
- 3rd Vermont
- 4th Vermont
- 5th Vermont
- 6th Vermont
- 11th Vermont (1st Heavy Artillery)

Second Brigade Brigadier General Frank Wheaton

- 62nd New York
- 93rd Pennsylvania
- 98th Pennsylvania
- 102nd Pennsylvania
- 139th Pennsylvania

Third Brigade Brigadier General Daniel Bidwell

- 7th Maine
- 29th New York
- 43rd New York
- 77th New York
- 122nd New York
- 61st Pennsylvania

Third Division—Brigadier General James H. Ricketts

First Brigade Colonel William Emerson

- 14th New Jersey
- 106th New York

151st New York
87th Pennsylvania
10th Vermont

Second Brigade Colonel Joseph Warren Kiefer
6th Maryland
9th New York Heavy Artillery (as infantry)
110th Ohio
122nd Ohio
126th Ohio
67th Pennsylvania
138th Pennsylvania

Artillery Brigade Colonel Charles H. Tompkins
5th Maine Light Battery
1st Massachusetts Light Artillery, Battery A
1st New York Independent Battery
1st Rhode Island Light Artillery, Battery C
1st Rhode Island Light Artillery, Battery G
5th U.S. Artillery, Battery M

XIX Corps—Major General William H. Emory

First Division—Brigadier General William Dwight

First Brigade Brigadier General George L. Beal
29th Maine
30th Massachusetts
114th New York
116th New York
153rd New York

Second Brigade Brigadier General James W. McMillan
12th Connecticut
160th New York
47th Pennsylvania
8th Vermont

Artillery

5th New York Independent Battery

Second Division—Brigadier General Cuvier Grover

First Brigade Brigadier General Henry W. Birge

9th Connecticut
12th Maine
14th Maine
26th Massachusetts
14th New Hampshire
75th New York

Second Brigade Colonel Edward L. Molineux

13th Connecticut
11th Indiana
22nd Iowa
3rd Massachusetts Cavalry (dismounted)
131st New York
159th New York

Third Brigade Colonel Jacob Sharpe (WIA); Lt. Colonel James P. Richardson (WIA); Lt. Colonel Alfred Neafie

38th Massachusetts
128th New York
156th New York
175th New York (3 companies)
176th New York

Fourth Brigade Colonel David Shunk

8th Indiana
18th Indiana
24th Iowa
28th Iowa

Artillery

1st Maine Light Battery

Reserve Artillery Captain Elijah Taft
- 17th Indiana Light Battery
- 1st Rhode Island Battery D

Army of West Virginia [VIII Corps]—Major General George Crook

First Division—Colonel Joseph Thoburn

First Brigade Colonel George D. Wells
- 34th Massachusetts
- 5th New York Heavy Artillery, 2nd Battalion (as infantry)
- 116th Ohio
- 123rd Ohio

Second Brigade (not engaged)

Third Brigade Colonel Thomas M. Harris
- 23rd Illinois
- 54th Pennsylvania
- 10th West Virginia
- 11th West Virginia
- 15th West Virginia

Second Division—Colonel Isaac H. Duval (WIA); Colonel Rutherford B. Hayes

First Brigade Colonel Rutherford B. Hayes; Colonel Hiram F. Devol
- 23rd Ohio
- 36th Ohio
- 5th West Virginia
- 13th West Virginia

Second Brigade Colonel Daniel D. Johnson (WIA); Lt. Colonel Benjamin F. Coates
- 34th Ohio
- 91st Ohio
- 9th West Virginia
- 14th West Virginia

Artillery Captain Henry A. DuPont
- 1st Ohio Light Artillery, Battery L
- 1st Pennsylvania Light Artillery, Battery I
- 5th U.S. Artillery, Battery B

Cavalry Corps Major General Alfred T.A. Torbert

First Division—Brigadier General Wesley Merritt

First Brigade Brigadier General George A. Custer
- 1st Michigan Cavalry
- 5th Michigan Cavalry
- 6th Michigan Cavalry
- 7th Michigan Cavalry
- 25th New York Cavalry

Second Brigade Brigadier General Thomas C. Devin
- 1st New York Dragoons
- 4th New York Dragoons
- 6th New York Cavalry
- 9th New York Cavalry
- 19th New York Cavalry
- 17th Pennsylvania Cavalry

Reserve Brigade Colonel Alfred Gibbs; Colonel Charles R. Lowell, Jr.
- 2nd Massachusetts Cavalry
- 6th Pennsylvania Cavalry [sent 9/8 to Pleasant Valley, Md.]
- 1st U.S. Cavalry
- 2nd U.S. Cavalry
- 5th U.S. Cavalry

Second Division—Brigadier General William W. Averell

First Brigade Colonel James M. Schoonmaker
- 8th Ohio Cavalry
- 14th Pennsylvania Cavalry
- 22nd Pennsylvania Cavalry

Second Brigade Colonel William H. Powell
- 1st New York (Lincoln Cavalry)

1st West Virginia Cavalry
2nd West Virginia Cavalry
3rd West Virginia Cavalry
5th U.S. Artillery, Battery L

Third Division—Brigadier General James H. Wilson

First Brigade Brigadier General John B. McIntosh; Lt. Colonel George A. Purington
1st Connecticut Cavalry
3rd New Jersey Cavalry
2nd New York Cavalry
5th New York Cavalry
2nd Ohio Cavalry
18th Pennsylvania Cavalry

Second Brigade Brigadier General George H. Chapman
3rd Indiana Cavalry (3 companies)
1st New Hampshire Cavalry Battalion
8th New York Cavalry
22nd New York Cavalry
1st Vermont Cavalry

Horse Artillery
1st U.S. Artillery, Batteries K & L
2nd U.S. Artillery, Batteries B & L
2nd U.S. Artillery, Battery D
3rd U.S. Artillery, Batteries C & F
4th U.S. Artillery, Battery C

Confederate
Army of the Valley District
Lt. General Jubal A. Early

Breckinridge's Corps—Major General John C. Breckenridge

Breckinridge's Division—Brigadier General Gabriel C. Wharton

Smith's Brigade—Colonel Thomas Smith
36th Virginia
45th Virginia Battalion

60th Virginia
69th North Carolina (Thomas' Legion)

Forsberg's Brigade—Colonel Augustus Forsberg (WIA)
30th Virginia Battalion Sharpshooters
45th Virginia
51st Virginia

Patton's Brigade—Colonel George S. Patton (MWIA)
22nd Virginia
23rd Virginia Battalion
26th Virginia Battalion

Gordon's Division—Major General John B. Gordon

Evans' Brigade—Colonel Edmund N. Atkinson
12th Georgia Battalion
13th Georgia
26th Georgia
31st Georgia
38th Georgia
60th Georgia
61st Georgia

Terry's Brigade—Brigadier General William Terry
2nd Virginia
4th Virginia
5th Virginia
27th Virginia
33rd Virginia

Colonel John H. S. Funk (MWIA)
21st Virginia
25th Virginia
42nd Virginia
44th Virginia
48th Virginia
50th Virginia

Colonel Robert H. Dungan

10th Virginia

23rd Virginia

37th Virginia

York's Brigade—Brigadier General Zebulon York (WIA)

Colonel William R. Peck

5th Louisiana

6th Louisiana

7th Louisiana

8th Louisiana

9th Louisiana

1st Louisiana

2nd Louisiana

10th Louisiana

14th Louisiana

15th Louisiana

Ramseur's Division—Major General Stephen D. Ramseur

Pegram's Brigade—Brigadier General John Pegram

13th Virginia

31st Virginia

49th Virginia

52nd Virginia

58th Virginia

Hoke's Brigade—Brigadier General Archibald Godwin (KIA); Lt. Colonel Anderson Ellis (WIA); Lt. Colonel William S. Davis

6th North Carolina

21st North Carolina

54th North Carolina

57th North Carolina

Johnston's Brigade—Brigadier General Robert D. Johnston

5th North Carolina

12th North Carolina

20th North Carolina
23rd North Carolina

Rodes' Division—Major General Robert E. Rodes (MWIA)

Battle's Brigade—Brigadier General Cullen A. Battle; Colonel Samuel B. Pickens (WIA); Colonel Charles Forsyth
3rd Alabama
5th Alabama
6th Alabama
12th Alabama
61st Alabama

Grimes' Brigade—Brigadier General Bryan Grimes
2nd North Carolina Battalion
32nd North Carolina
43rd North Carolina
45th North Carolina
53rd North Carolina

Cook's Brigade—Brigadier General Philip Cook
4th Georgia
12th Georgia
21st Georgia
44th Georgia

Cox's Brigade—Colonel William R. Cox
1st North Carolina
2nd North Carolina
3rd North Carolina
4th North Carolina
14th North Carolina
30th North Carolina

Cavalry—Major General Fitzhugh Lee

Lee's Division—Brigadier General Williams Wickham

Lomax's Brigade—Colonel Reuben Boston, Colonel William Payne
- 5th Virginia Cavalry
- 6th Virginia Cavalry
- 15th Virginia Cavalry

Wickham's Brigade—Colonel Thomas Owen; Colonel Thomas Munford
- 1st Virginia Cavalry
- 2nd Virginia Cavalry
- 3rd Virginia Cavalry
- 4th Virginia Cavalry

Horse Artillery—Major James Breathed
- 1st Stuart Horse Artillery
- Lynchburg Beauregard Artillery

Lomax's Division—Major General Lunsford L. Lomax

Imboden's Brigade—Colonel George H. Smith
- 18th Virginia Cavalry
- 23rd Virginia Cavalry
- 62nd Virginia Mounted Infantry

Johnson's Brigade—Major General Bradley Johnson
- 1st Maryland Cavalry Battalion
- 2nd Maryland Cavalry Battalion
- 8th Virginia Cavalry
- 21st Virginia Cavalry
- 27th Virginia Cavalry Battalion
- 36th Virginia Cavalry Battalion
- 37th Virginia Cavalry Battalion

McCausland's Brigade—Brigadier General John C. McCausland; Colonel Milton Ferguson
- 14th Virginia Cavalry
- 16th Virginia Cavalry
- 17th Virginia Cavalry
- 22nd Virginia Cavalry

Jackson's Brigade—Lt. Colonel William P. Thompson
- 19th Virginia Cavalry
- 20th Virginia Cavalry
- 46th Virginia Cavalry Battalion
- 47th Virginia Cavalry Battalion

Vaughn's Brigade—Brigadier General John C. Vaughn (not engaged)

Artillery—Colonel Thomas H. Carter

Braxton's Battalion—Major Carter M. Braxton
- Allegheny Battery
- Lee Battery
- Stafford Battery

McLaughlin's Battalion—Lt. Colonel J. Floyd King
- Lewisburg Artillery
- Monroe Battery
- Wise Legion Battery

Nelson's Battalion—Major William Nelson
- Amherst Battery
- Fluvanna Artillery
- Georgia Regular Battery

CHAPTER 5

ADDITIONAL SITES

Free self-guided walking tour brochures for downtown Winchester are available at the Winchester-Frederick County Visitor's Center and Old Town Welcome Center. For further information, inquire at the Old Town Development Board, (540) 535-3661; the Winchester-Frederick County Visitor's Center, (540) 542-1326; the Winchester-Frederick Historical Society, (540) 662-6550; or Preservation of Historic Winchester, (540) 665-3577.

The Stonewall Cemetery

Mount Hebron Cemetery, (540) 662-4868, is located at 305 E. Boscawen St. The Stonewall Confederate Cemetery is located within.

Mt. Hebron Cemetery Gate

The imposing entrance to Mount Hebron, Winchester's oldest cemetery, leads directly to the Stonewall Confederate Cemetery established by the Ladies Memorial Association in 1866. Among the marked graves here are those for the Ashby and Patton brothers. Confederate Memorial Day has been celebrated here every June 6 since 1866. [Bob Price]

Stonewall Confederate Cemetery

[Bob Price]

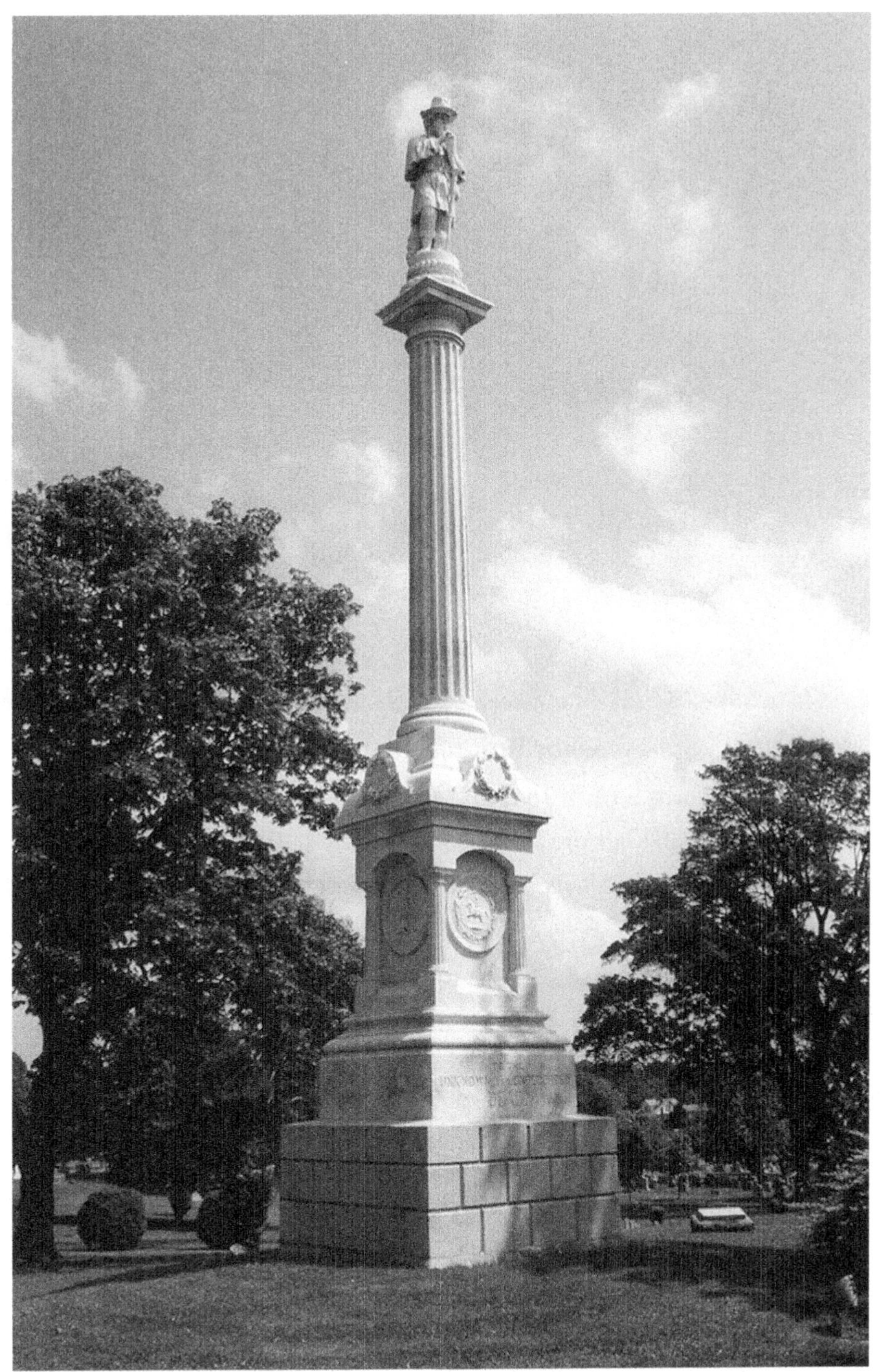

Unknown Confederate Dead statue

Towering over the graves of the Confederate dead is the Italian-made monument to the unknown dead. It was dedicated in 1879. [Bob Price]

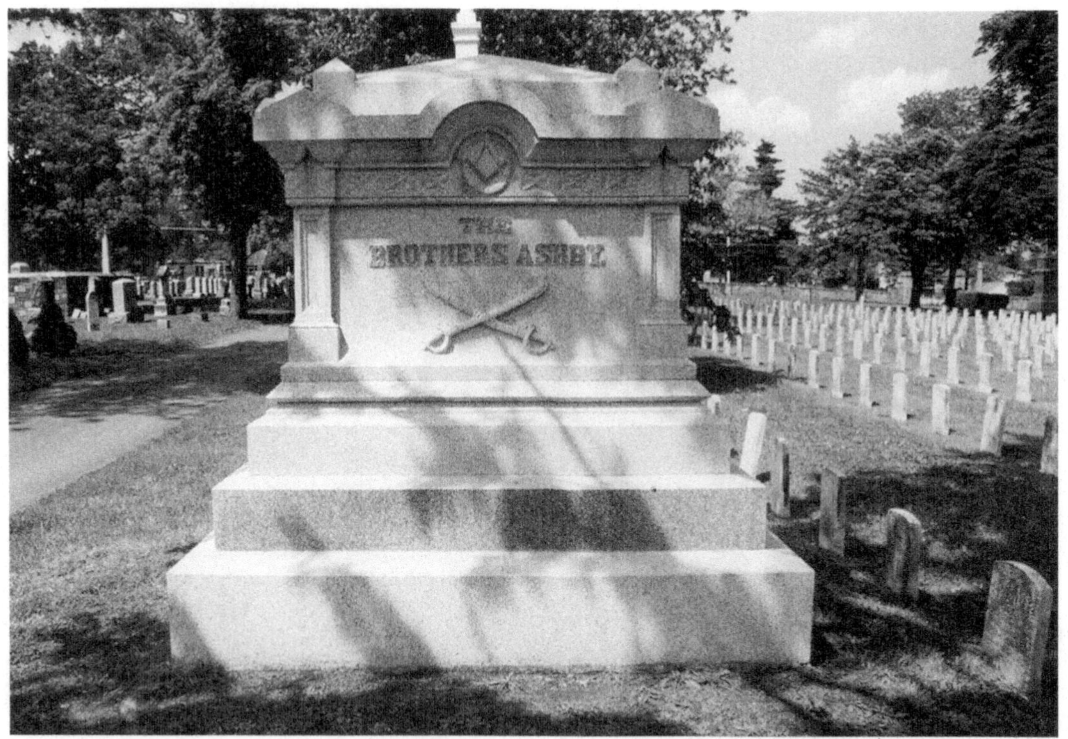

Ashby Brothers monument

Richard Ashby was KIA in 1861 and Brigadier General Turner Ashby was KIA in June 1862. They are buried side by side. If Turner had survived he might have been as famous a cavalry commander as Jeb Stuart. [Bob Price]

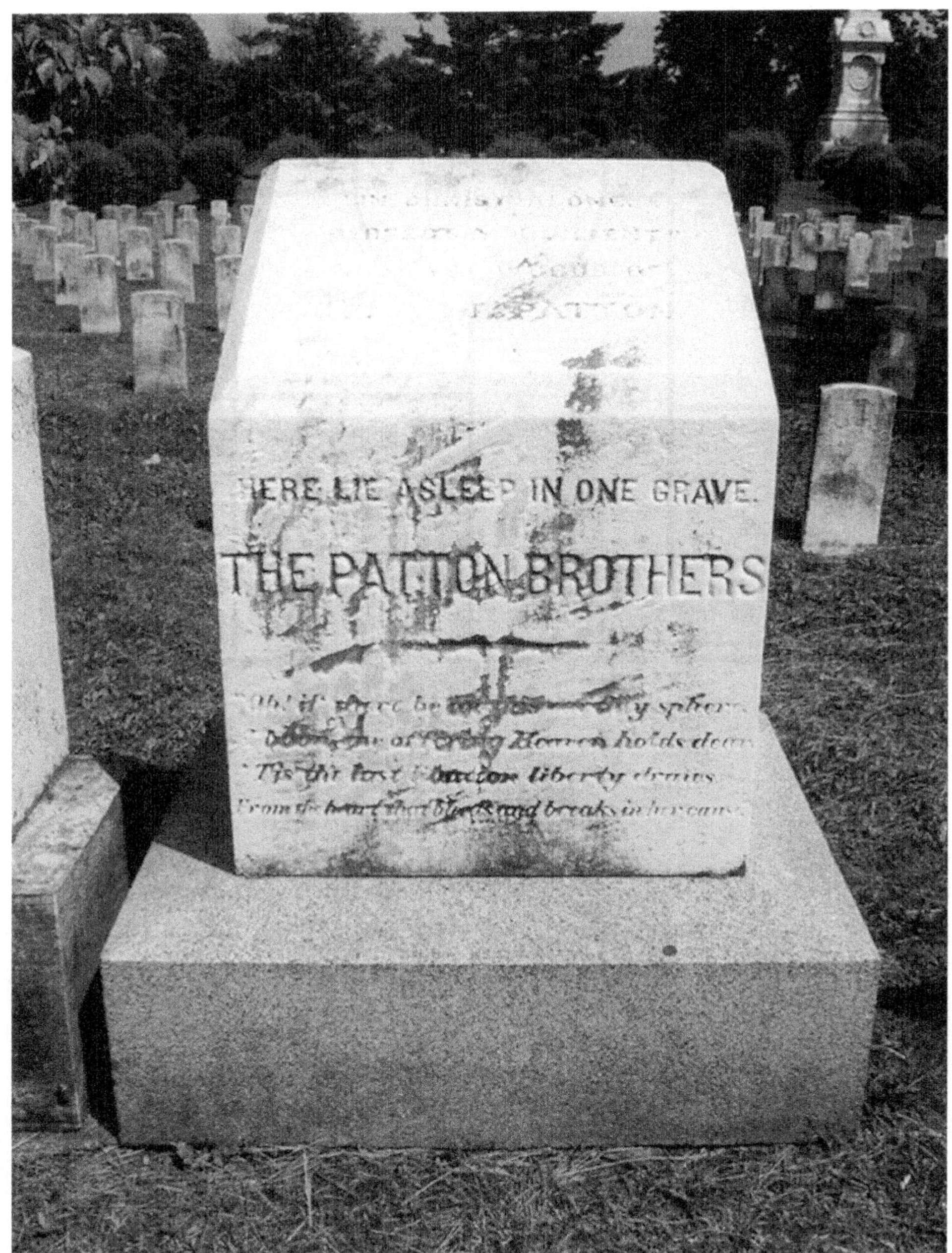

Patton Brothers monument

Resting place for Colonel George S. Patton who was mortally wounded at the Third Battle of Winchester. The other brother buried here is Colonel Waller Tazewell Patton who was KIA at Gettysburg on July 3, 1863. WWII general George S. Patton, Jr., was the grandson of the former. [Bob Price]

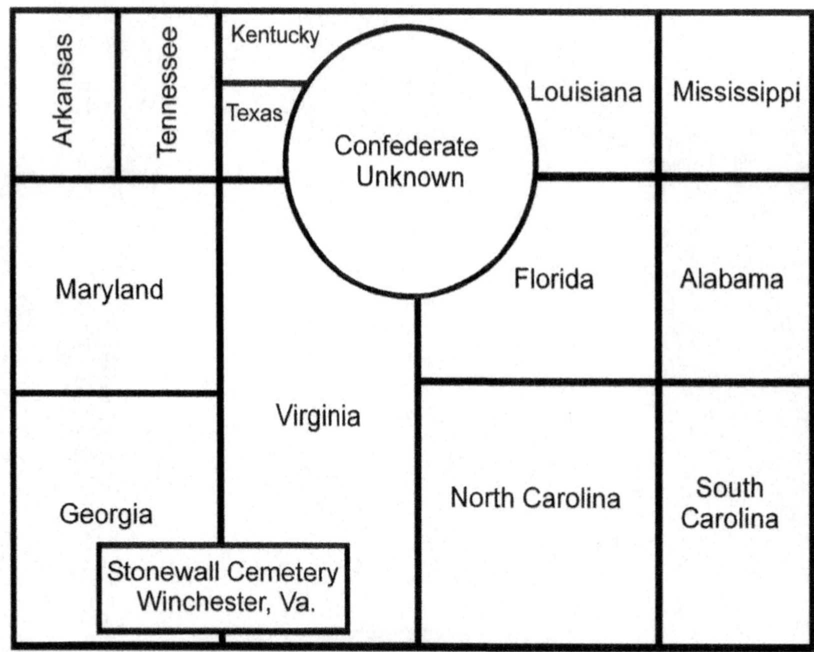

Stonewall Confederate Cemetery map

[Jonathan Noyalas]

The essential introduction and guide to Winchester's Confederate legacy is Jonathan Noyalas' article "After the Storm" in the Winchester-Frederick County Historical Society's *Journal* Vol. XVIII, 2006, pp. 93–119.

There is a roster of Confederates buried here. See "A Roster of Confederate Soldiers Buried in the Stonewall Cemetery," Lucy Kurtz and Ben Ritter, for the Turner Ashby Chapter of the United Daughters of the Confederacy.

In the summer of 1865, Mary Dunbar Williams organized the Ladies' Aid Society to begin the vast effort of recovering and re-interring the Confederate dead who lie here, known and unknown. In all, 2,575 Confederate soldiers, from every state in the Confederacy, are buried here.

The cemetery is one of Winchester's most beautiful sites. The cemetery is maintained now with the help of the Turner Ashby Chapter of the United Daughters of the Confederacy. Every June 6, since 1866, the chapter decorates the Cemetery and each soldier's grave with Confederate and state banners. It is a beautiful setting for the evening memorial service.

Confederate Memorial Day 1914

Winchester has held a Confederate Memorial Day every June 6 since 1866. In years past, Confederate veterans marched on Loudoun Street. Here, in 1914, Confederate veterans from the Turner Ashby Camp, United Confederate Veterans are passing by the Taylor Hotel on Loudoun Street. Winchester's last Confederate veteran died in 1943. [Handley Library Collection, Stewart Bell, Jr. Archives Room, Handley Regional Library, Winchester, VA]

As you approach the Stonewall Cemetery, the first state monument you will see is from South Carolina. Nearby is the grave of General John G. Walker. Next are the North Carolina monument and the grave of General Robert Johnston, who fought in the Third Battle of Winchester. He lies close to "The Brothers Ashby," Turner and Richard, and the Patton brothers. Colonel Waller T. Patton was mortally wounded at Gettysburg in 1863, and Colonel George S. Patton met the same fate at Winchester in 1864. The Pattons were, respectively, the great uncle and the grandfather of General George S. Patton, who served his country in World War II.

The Virginia and Georgia monuments complete the front rank of markers; behind them, and flanking the towering Unknown Soldier (c.1879), are monuments from Alabama, Florida, Louisiana, Maryland, Mississippi, Tennessee, and Arkansas.

In 1999, the Ladies' Confederate Memorial Association and the Turner Ashby Chapter of the United Daughters of the Confederacy dedicated the monument honoring the Women of Winchester.

Old Court House Civil War Museum
20 N. Loudoun St.
(540) 542-1145
www.civilwarmuseum.org

Hours:
May 1 through October 31:
Monday through Saturday 10 AM to 5 PM
Sunday 1 PM to 5 PM

November 1 through April 30:
Wednesday through Saturday 10 AM to 5 PM
Sunday 1 PM to 5 PM

Admission: $5
Children, Senior and Group Discounts

Confederate veterans from the Turner Ashby Camp, UCV

They are standing on the steps of the Frederick County Court House in 1895. [WFCHS Collection, Stewart Bell, Jr. Archives Room, Handley Regional Library, Winchester, VA]

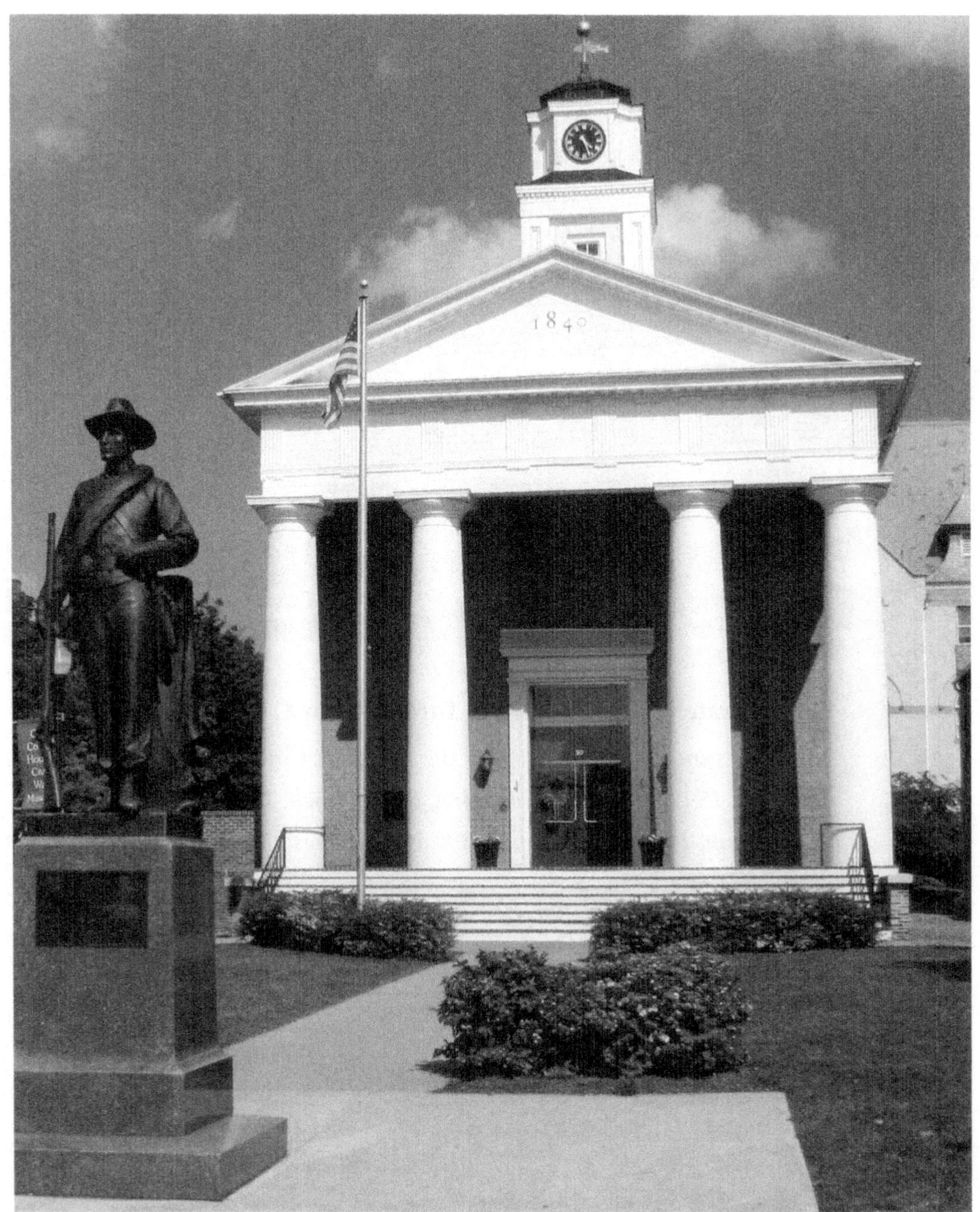

Old Court House Civil War Museum today

Formerly the Frederick County Court House. The museum is operated by the Shenandoah Valley Battlefields Foundation (SVBF). [Bob Price]

The courthouse, built in 1840, served as a wartime prison and hospital. In 1996 Frederick County took the lead in developing the building as a Civil War Museum. Harry and Trish Ridgeway then created a nationally recognized collection of artifacts and photographs illustrating the lives of common soldiers, Union and Confederate. The museum now is operated by the Shenandoah Valley Battlefields Foundation [SVBF].

The Taylor Hotel
125 N. Loudoun St.

Taylor Hotel from about 1906

[Handley Library Collection, Stewart Bell, Jr. Archives Room, Handley Regional Library, Winchester, VA]

Taylor Hotel today

[John Fox]

The Taylor Hotel, 125 N. Loudoun St., was constructed circa 1846. The hotel is one of Winchester's most venerable buildings. It is an important part of Winchester's Civil War heritage. It was Stonewall Jackson's first headquarters in Winchester and in May 1862, Jackson presented Turner Ashby with his promotion to the rank of brigadier general.

The middle section collapsed in 2007, and the remainder was condemned. But thanks to the City of Winchester's Economic Development Authority, restoration work began in 2012. The iconic three-story porch has been recreated.

The "Fourth Battle of Winchester"—the battle for historic preservation—is still with us. There have been both irreparable losses and significant victories. Historical consciousness and preservation energy have never been higher than they are today. Many of posterity's losses and gains alike have been noted in these pages. Despite important losses we can agree with Paul Hawkes, who in 2009 was the Director of the National Park Services Battlefield Preservation Program:

> This land returns enough of its historic character that the men who fought here would recognize its features.

Hawkes was speaking specifically about the Middle Field on today's Shenandoah Valley Battlefields Foundation Third Battle site. The same could be said for many other Winchester and Frederick County battlefields. Milburn Lane though, stands out as a spot that today [2016] still retains its historical look from the 1860s. Between the cemetery and the bridge time seems to have stopped. No soldier from either army, that I know of, ever wrote a description—it was too typical of where they came from, too ordinary—to merit a description. But there is nothing ordinary about it today. It's the one Winchester site common to all three battles. Jackson ended his pursuit of Banks here. Over 4,000 of Milroy's men surrendered here, ending the Second Battle. The great cavalry assault that ended the Third Battle began here.

Preservation begins with and builds on education. When people come face to face with facts in a little changed landscape then the sacrifices made by these ordinary soldiers become crystal clear. The soldiers who wore blue and gray all gave up the comforts of their homes and families. Many gave their lives, in victory or in defeat. Come to Milburn Lane to understand the sacrifices. Winning the Fourth Battle of Winchester demands education, restraint, and respect from all of us.

BIBLIOGRAPHY

Primary Sources

Allen, William. *History of the Campaign of Gen. T. J. (Stonewall) Jackson in the Shenandoah Valley of Virginia from November 4, 1861 to June 17, 1862.* Dayton, Ohio: Morningside Bookshop, 1974.

A Memorial of the Great Rebellion: Being a History of the 14th Regiment New Hampshire Volunteers. Boston: Franklin Press, n.d.

Anderson, R. P. *Genealogy: Spaid, Anderson, Whitacre and a Number of Allied Families.* Also, *Historical Facts and Memories.* Strasburg, Va.: Shenandoah Publishing, Inc., 1975.

Andrews, Matthew Page, ed. *The Women of the South in War Times.* Baltimore: The Norman, Remington Co., 1920.

Andrews, Richard Snowden. *A Memoir.* Baltimore: The Sun Printing Office, 1910.

Baker, I. N. "Diary and Recollections of I. Norvell Baker." *Diaries, Letters, and Recollections of the War Between the States*, 96–128. Edited by Garland Quarles et al. Winchester, Va.: Winchester-Frederick County Historical Society, 1955.

Bennett, A. J. *The Story of the First Massachusetts Light Battery.* Boston: Deland and Barta, 1886.

Brinton, John H. *Personal Memoirs of John H. Brinton.* New York: Neale Publishing Co., 1914.

Carpenter, G. N. *History of the Eighth Regiment Vermont Volunteers, 1861–1865.* Boston: Deland and Barta, 1886.

Carter, Thomas Henry Letters. John Warwick Daniel Papers, D.M. Rubenstein Rare Book and Manuscript Library, Duke University, Durham, NC. [letters date 11/19/1894 & 11/28/1894].

Casler, John O. *Four Years in the Stonewall Brigade*. Dayton, Ohio: Morningside Press, 1982.

Chase, Julia. "Record of the Various Occupations of Winchester: As Set Down in the Diary of Miss Julia Chase." In *Diaries, Letters, and Recollections of the War Between the States*, 9–13. Edited by Garland Quarles et al. Winchester, Va.: Winchester-Frederick County Historical Society, 1955.

Clark, Walter, ed. *Histories of the Several Regiments and Battalions from North Carolina in the Civil War, 1861–1865*. Raleigh: E. M. Uzzell, 1901.

Colt, Margaretta Barton. *Defend the Valley: A Shenandoah Family in the Civil War.* New York: Crown Publishers, Inc., 1994.

Crook, George. *General George Crook: His Autobiography.* Edited by M.F. Schmitt. Norman, Ok.: University of Oklahoma Press, 1960.

Davidson, Garber A., ed. *The Civil War Letters of the Late 1st Lieut. James J. Hartley, 122nd Ohio Infantry Regiment*. Jefferson, N.C.: McFarland and Co., 1998.

Davis, Edwin A., ed. "A Louisiana Volunteer: Letters of William J. Walter, 1861–1862." *Southern Review* (1933): 78–87.

DeForest, John W. *A Volunteer's Adventures: A Union Captain's Record of the Civil War.* Edited by J. H. Croushore. New York: Archon Books, 1970.

Duncan, Richard R. *Alexander Neil and the Last Shenandoah Valley Campaign: Letter of an Army Surgeon to His Family, 1864*. Shippensburg, Pa.: White Mane Publishing, 1996.

Early, Jubal A. *A Memoir of the Last Year of the War for Independence in the Confederate States of America*. Lynchburg, Va.: Charles W. Button, 1867.

_______. *War Memoirs: Autobiographical Sketch and Narrative of the War Between the States*. Edited by Frank E. Vandiver. Bloomington: Indiana University Press, 1960.

Eby, Cecil D., Jr., ed. *A Virginia Yankee in the Civil War: The Diaries of David Hunter Strother.* Chapel Hill, N.C.: University of North Carolina Press, 1961.

Ewell, R. S. *The Making of a Soldier: Letters of General R. S. Ewell*. Edited by Captain Percy Gatling Hamlin. Richmond, Va.: Whittet and Shepperson, 1935.

Gilmor, Colonel Harry. *Four Years in the Saddle.* New York: Harper & Brothers, 1866.

Goldsborough, W. W. *The Maryland Line in the Confederate Army, 1861–1865.* Baltimore: Guggenheimer, Weil & Co., 1900.

Gordon, John B. *Reminiscences of the Civil War.* New York: Charles Scribner's Sons, 1904.

Harriet H. Griffith Diary, August 21, 1861, [208] Winchester-Frederick County Historical Society, Stewart Bell, Jr. Archives, Handley Regional Library, Winchester Va.

Hale, Laura Virginia, and Stanley S. Phillips. *History of the Forty-Ninth Virginia Infantry C.S.A.* "Extra Billy Smith's Boys." Based upon unpublished memoirs of Captain Robert Daniel Funkhouser, "Warren Blues," Company D, 49th Virginia Infantry, C.S.A. Lanham, Md.: S. S. Phillips, 1981.

Haines, A. H. *History of the 15th Regiment*, New Jersey Volunteers. New York: Jenkins and Thomas, 1883.

Hotchkiss, Jedediah. *Make Me a Map of the Valley: The Civil War Journal of Stonewall Jackson's Topographer.* Edited by Archie P. McDonald. Dallas: Southern Methodist University Press, 1973.

Humphreys, Milton. Humphrey's Civil War Diary. Sept. 1864. Special Collections Department, Alderman Library, Alderman Library, University of Virginia, Charlottesville, Va.

Isham, Asa. *An Historical Sketch of the 7th Regiment, Michigan Volunteer Cavalry.* New York: Town Topics, 1893.

Jackson, Mary Anna. *Memoirs of "Stonewall" Jackson.* Dayton, Ohio: Morningside, 1993.

Jones, Terry L., ed. *The Civil War Memoirs of Captain William J. Seymour: Reminiscences of a Louisiana Tiger.* Baton Rouge: Louisiana State University Press, 1991.

Jordan, Leonard. *History of the 1st, 10th, 29th Maine Regiments.* Portland, Maine: Steven Berg, 1871.

King, John R. *My Experience in the Confederate Army and in Northern Prisons.* Clarksburg, W. Va.: Stonewall Jackson Chapter, U.D.C., 1917.

Lanthrop, Barnes, ed. "An Autobiography of Francis T. Nicholls." *The Louisiana Historical Quarterly* 17 (1934): 246–67.

Lynch, Charles H. *The Civil War Diary of Charles H. Lynch, 18th Connecticut Volunteers.* n.p., 1918.

Mahon, Michael G., ed. *Winchester Divided: The Civil War Diaries of Julia Chase and Laura Lee.* Harrisburg, Pa.: Stackpole Books, 2002.

McDonald, Cornelia. *A Diary: With Reminiscences of the War and Refugee Life in the Shenandoah Valley, 1860–1865.* Nashville: Cullom & Ghertner, 1934.

McDonald, Cornelia Peake. *A Woman's Civil War: A Diary with Reminiscences of the War, from March 1862.* Gwin, Minrose C., ed. Madison: University of Wisconsin Press, 1992.

McKim, R. H. *A Soldier's Recollections.* New York: Longman, Green and Co., 1910.

Moore, Edward A. *The Story of a Cannoneer under Stonewall Jackson.* Lynchburg, Va.: J. P. Bell Co., Inc., 1910.

Munford, T. T. "Reminiscences of Cavalry Operations." *Southern Historical Society Papers* 12 (1884) and 13 (1885).

Nichols, G. W. *A Soldier's Story of His Regiment (61st Georgia).* Kennesaw, Ga.: Continental Book Co., 1961.

Quint, Alonzo. *The Second Massachusetts Infantry.* Boston: James Walker, 1867.

Ronge, William H., ed. *Four Years in the Confederate Artillery: The Diary of Private Henry Robinson Berkeley.* Richmond: Virginia Historical Society, 1991.

Sheridan, P. H. *Personal Memoirs of P. H. Sheridan.* New York: C. L. Webster, 1888.

Sperry, Kate. *Surrender? Never Surrender.* Typewritten manuscript of a war-time diary. Handley Library Archives, Winchester, Va.

Starr, Stephen Z., ed. "Winter Quarters Near Winchester, 1864–1865: Reminiscences of Roger Hannaford, Second Ohio Cavalry." *Virginia Magazine of History and Biography,* 86 (3): 320–38.

Stiles, Robert. *Four Years under Marse Robert.* New York: Neale Publishing Co., 1903.

Sutton, J. J. *History of the 2nd Regiment West Virginia Volunteers During the War of the Rebellion.* Portsmouth, Ohio: n.p., 1892.

Taylor, Richard. *Destruction and Reconstruction: Personal Experiences of the Late War.* New York: D. Appleton and Co., 1879.

Tobie, E. P. *History of the First Maine Cavalry, 1861–1865.* Boston: Emery and Hughes, 1887.

Turner, Charles W., ed. "Major Charles A. Davidson: Letters of a Virginia Soldier." *Civil War History* 22 (1976): 16–40.

Tyler, M. W. *Recollections of the Civil War.* New York: G. P. Putnam's, 1912.

Vaill, T. H. *History of the 2nd Connecticut Volunteer Heavy Artillery.* Winsted, Conn.: Winsted Printing Co., 1868.

_______. *The County Regiment: A Sketch of the 2nd Regiment of Connecticut Volunteer Heavy Artillery.* Originally *The 19th Volunteer Infantry in the Civil War.* Litchfield County: Conn.: University Club, 1908.

Walker, W. C. *History of the Eighteenth Regiment Connecticut Volunteers in the War for the Union.* Norwich, Conn.: The Committee, 1885.

Wall, H. C. *Historical Sketch of the Pee Dee Guards (Company D, 23rd North Carolina Regiment) from 1861 to 1865.* Raleigh, N.C.: Edwards, Broughton and Co., 1876.

Secondary Sources

Allan, William. *History of the Campaign of General T. J. (Stonewall) Jackson in the Shenandoah Valley of Virginia.* Dayton, Ohio: Morningside Press, 1991.

Allen, T. Harrel. *Lee's Last Major General: Bryan Grimes of North Carolina.* Mason City, La.: Savas Publishing, 1999.

Avirett, Rev. James E. *The Memoirs of General Turner Ashby.* Baltimore: Selby & Dulaney, 1867.

Beck, Brandon H., ed. *Civil War Battles 1861–1865: Winchester and Frederick County, Virginia.* Winchester, Va.: Winchester-Frederick County Historical Society, 2002.

_______. "Marches Into the Unknown." Winchester: Winchester-Frederick County Historical Society Journal, XVII, 2005, pp : 39–47.

_______. "Reflections at Stephenson, Virginia." *Crossroads to History* 3, no. 9 (September 1998) : 9–14.

_______. "Stonewall in Winchester." *Crossroads to History* 1, no. 1 (July–August 1996): 3–4.

_______. *The Second Battle of Winchester: June 12–15, 1863.* Lynchburg, Va.: H. E. Howard, Inc., 1989.

_______. "The Second Battle of Winchester." *Potomac Magazine* (Spring 1994): 44–48.

_______. ed. *Third Alabama: The Civil War Memoir of Brigadier General Cullen Andrews Battle, C.S.A.* Tuscaloosa, AL.: University of Alabama Press, 2000.

Beck, Brandon H., and Charles Grunder. *Jackson's Valley Campaign: The First Battle of Winchester.* Lynchburg, Va.: H. E. Howard, Inc., 1992.

Beck, Brandon H. and Charles S. Grunder *Three Battles of Winchester: A History and Guided Tour.* Berryville: The Civil War Foundation, 1997.

Beck, Brandon H., and Roger Delauter, Jr. *The Third Battle of Winchester.* Lynchburg, Va.: H. E. Howard, Inc., 1997.

Beck, Brandon H., and Rebecca Ebert, Todd Kern, Richard Kleese, Ben Ritter, and Joseph Whitehorne. *Standing Ground: The Civil War in the Shenandoah Valley.* Winchester: The Northern Virginia Daily, 1996.

Breeden, James O. "An Island of Hope in a Sea of Misery: Confederate Winchester and the Humane Treatment of Prisoners of War." Non-published speech, 1992.

Bushong, M. K. *General Turner Ashby and Stonewall's Valley Campaign.* Verona, Va.: McClure Printing Co., 1980.

_______. *Old Jube: A Biography of General Jubal A. Early.* Boyce, Va.: Carr Publishing Co., 1955.

Cartmell, T. K. *Shenandoah Valley Pioneers and Their Descendants: A History of Frederick County, Virginia from Its Formation in 1738 to 1908*. Berryville, Va.: Chesapeake Book Co., 1963.

Cohn, D. A. *Jackson's Valley Campaign*. Washington, D.C.: American Publishing Co., 1986.

Collins, Darrell L. *Major General Robert E. Rodes of the Army of Northern Virginia*. New York: Savas Beatie, 2009.

Cooling, B. F. *Jubal Early's Raid on Washington, 1864*. Baltimore: The National & Aviation Publishing Company of America, 1989.

Cozzens, Peter. *Shenandoah 1862: Stonewall Jackson's Valley Campaign*. Chapel Hill: University of North Carolina Press, 2008.

Davis, Burke. *They Called Him Stonewall*. New York: Rinehard & Co., 1954.

Davis, James A. *51st Virginia Infantry*. Lynchburg, Va.: H. E. Howard, Inc., 1984.

Delauter, Roger. *The Eighteenth Virginia Cavalry*. Lynchburg: H.E. Howard, Inc., 1985.

Delauter, Roger U., Jr. *Winchester in the Civil War*. Lynchburg, Va.: H. E. Howard, Inc., 1992.

Douglas, Henry Kyd. *I Rode with Stonewall*. Edited by John Kyd Beckenbaugh. Chapel Hill, N.C.: University of North Carolina Press, 1940.

Dowdey, Clifford, and Manarin, Louis, eds. *The Wartime Papers of R.E. Lee*. Richmond: Commonwealth of Virginia, 1961.

Ecelbarger, Gary. *Three Days in the Shenandoah: Stonewall Jackson at Front Royal and Winchester*. Norman, Ok.: University of Oklahoma Press, 2008.

________. *"We Are In For It" The First Battle of Kernstown, March 23, 1862*. Shippensburg, Pa.: White Mane Pub., 1997.

Eby, Cecil D. Jr. *"Porte Crayon," The Life of David Hunter Strother*. Chapel Hill, N.C.: University of North Carolina Press, 1961.

Freeman, Douglas Southall. *Lee's Lieutenants*. New York: Charles Scribner's Sons, 1943.

_______. *R. E. Lee*. New York: Charles Scribner's Sons, 1935–36.

Gallagher, Gary W. *Stephen Dodson Ramseur: Lee's Gallant General*. Chapel Hill, N.C.: University of North Carolina Press, 1985.

Greene, A. Wilson. *Whatever You Resolve to Be: Essays on Stonewall Jackson*. Baltimore: Butternut & Blue, 1992.

Hale, Laura V. *Four Valiant Years in the Lower Shenandoah, 1861–1865*. Strasburg, Va.: Shenandoah Publishing House, 1973.

Hamlin, P. G. *Old Bald Head, General R. S. Ewell: The Portrait of a Soldier*. Strasburg, Va.: Shenandoah Publishing House, 1940.

Hassler, William. "Dr. McGuire's Contribution to Military Medicine." Winchester, Va.: Winchester-Frederick County Historical Association Journal, XVI, 2004, p. 85–73.

Heatwole, John L. *The Burning: Sheridan in the Shenandoah Valley*. Charlottesville, Va.: Rockbridge Publishing, 1998.

Hawkins, M. L. "Sketch of the Battle of Winchester, September 19, 1864." In *Sketches of War History: 1861–1865*. Cincinnati: Robert Clarke & Co., 1888.

Holsworth, Jerry W. "Quiet Courage: Winchester, Virginia in the Civil War." *Blue & Gray* 15, no. 2 (December 1997): 6–32.

_______. Jerry W. *Stonewall Jackson and Winchester, Virginia*. Charleston, S.C.: The History Press, 2012.

Hurst, Lora Ruth. *The Effect of Military Operations on Civil Life in Winchester, Virginia During the Civil War*. Master's Thesis, Kent State University, 1953.

Johnson, Clint. *In the Footsteps of Stonewall Jackson*. Winston Salem, N.C.: John Blair, 2002.

Johnston, A. J., II. *Virginia Railroads in the Civil War*. Chapel Hill, N.C.: University of North Carolina Press, 1961.

Johnston, Wilbur S. *The Battles of Milburn*. Winchester, Va.: Winchester Frederick County Historical Association, 2012.

Jones, Terry L. "Going Back into the Union at Last…" *Civil War Times Illustrated* 29 (January–February 1991): 55–60.

_______. *Lee's Tigers: The Louisiana Infantry in the Army of Northern Virginia.* Baton Rouge: Louisiana State University Press, 1987.

Kernstown Battlefield Association. *The First and Second Battles of Kernstown.* Pritchard—Grim Farm. Shenandoah Valley Battlefields Foundation and the National Park Service, 2004.

Kurtz, Lucy Fitzhugh, and Benny Ritter. *A Roster of Confederate Soldiers Buried in the Stonewall Cemetery, Winchester, Virginia.* Winchester, Va.: Farmers and Merchants National Bank, 1962.

Lehman, Sam. *The Story of Frederick County.* Winchester, Va.: Sam Lehman, n.d.

Lewis, Thomas. *The Shenandoah in Flames: The Valley Campaign of 1864.* Alexandria, Va.: Time-Life Books, 1987.

Levine, Bruce. *Confederate Emancipation: Southern Plans to Free and Arm Slaves During the Civil War.* New York: Oxford University Press, 2008.

Livermore, Thomas L. *Numbers and Losses in the Civil War in America: 1861–65.* Bloomington: Indiana University Press, 1957.

Lord, Walter, ed. *The Fremantle Diary.* New York: Capricorn Books, 1954.

Maier, Larry B. *Gateway to Gettysburg: The Second Battle of Winchester.* Shippensburg, Pa.: Burd Street Press, 2002.

_______. *Leather and Steel: The Twelfth Pennsylvania Cavalry in the Civil War.* Shippensburg, Pa.: Burd Street Press, 2002.

Merritt, General Wesley "Sheridan in the Shenandoah Valley." *Battles and Leaders of the Civil War, II.* New York: Thomas Yoseloff, 1958. pp. 500–522.

Miller, Edward A., Jr. *Lincoln's Abolitionist General: The Biography of David Hunter.* Columbia, S.C.: University of South Carolina Press, 1997.

Miller, William J. *Mapping for Stonewall: The Civil War Service of Jed Hotchkiss.* Washington: Elliot & Clark Publishing, 1993.

Miroff, Nick. "Saving a Civil War legacy in Virginia's Shenandoah Valley." *The Washington Post,* November 14, 2008.

Northcott, Robert S. (Lt. Col. 12th West Virginia Volunteers) " Milroy at Winchester," in *The New Annals of the Civil War*, Peter Cozzens & Girardi, Robert, eds. Mechanicsburg, Pa.: Stackpole Books, 2004.

Noyalas, Jonathan A. "After the Storm: Winchester's Civil War Legacy and Confederate Memory." Winchester, Va.: Winchester-Frederick County Historical Society Journal, v. 18, 2006, p. 93–119.

_______. "The Confederate Military Service of Private Robert T. Barton, 1861–1862," Winchester, Va.: Winchester-Frederick County Historical Association Journal, v. 16, 2004. p. 73–95.

_______. "Early's Costliest Victory: The Second Battle of Kernstown and Its Impact on Union Strategy in the Shenandoah Valley, 1864." Winchester-Frederick County Historical Society Journal, v. 15: p. 64–80.

Noyalas, Jonathan A., ed. *"Give the Enemy No Rest!" Sheridan's 1864 Shenandoah Campaign*. New Market, Va.: Shenandoah Valley Battlefields Foundation, 2007.

_______. *"My Will is Absolute Law:" A Biography of Union General Robert H. Milroy*: Jefferson, N.C.: McFarland and Company, 2006.

_______. *Plagued by War: Winchester, Virginia, During the Civil War*. Leesburg, Va.: Gauley Mount Press, 2003.

_______. *Stonewall Jackson's 1862 Valley Campaign: War Comes to the Homefront*. Charleston, S.C.: The History Press, 2003.

_______. "The Most Hated Man in Winchester." *America's Civil War* 17, no. 1 (March 2004): 30–36.

O'Connor, Adrian. Valley Pike column, "Star Fort." *Winchester Star*. September 12, 2007.

Parrish, T. Michael. *Richard Taylor: Soldier Prince of Dixie*. Chapel Hill, N.C.: University of North Carolina Press, 1994.

Patchan, Scott. *The Last Battle of Winchester: Phil Sheridan, Jubal Early and the Shenandoah Valley Campaign. August 7–September 19, 1864*. El Dorado Hills, California: Savas Beatie, 2013.

Pfanz, Donald. *Richard S. Ewell: A Soldier's Life*. Chapel Hill, N.C.: University of North Carolina Press, 1998.

Phillips, Edward H. *The Shenandoah Valley in 1864: An Episode in the History of Warfare*. Charleston, S.C.: The Citadel, 1965.

_______. *The Lower Shenandoah Valley in the Civil War: The Impact of the Civil War Upon the Civilian Population and Upon Civil Institutions*. Lynchburg, Va.: H.E. Howard, Inc., 1993

Phipps, Sheila R. *Genteel Rebel: The Life of Mary Greenhow Lee*. Baton Rouge: Louisiana State University Press, 2004.

Pope, Thomas E. *The Weary Boys: Colonel J. Warren Keifer and the 110th Ohio Volunteer Infantry*. Kent, Ohio: Kent State University Press, 2002.

Power, J. Tracy. *Lee's Miserables: Life in the Army of Northern Virginia from the Wilderness to Appomattox*. Chapel Hill, N.C.: University of North Carolina Press, 1998.

Prowell, George R. *History of the Eighty-Seventh Pennsylvania Volunteers*. York, Pa.: Press of the York Daily, 1903.

Quarles, Garland. *Civil War Battles in Winchester and Frederick County, Virginia*. Winchester: Civil War Centennial Commission, 1960.

_______. *Occupied Winchester*. Winchester, Va.: Farmers and Merchants National Bank, 1976.

_______. *Some Old Homes in Frederick County, Virginia*. Winchester, Va.: Farmers and Merchants National Bank, 1971.

_______. *The Story of 100 Old Homes in Winchester, Virginia*. Winchester, Va.: Farmers and Merchants National Bank, 1967.

Rankin, Thomas M. *Stonewall Jackson's Romney Campaign: January 1–February 20, 1862*. Lynchburg, Va.: H. E. Howard, Inc., 1994.

Ritter, Ben. "A Favorite Portrait of Stonewall." *Civil War Times Illustrated* 17 (1979): 36–39.

Robertson, James, I., Jr. *Civil War Sites in Virginia: A Tour Guide*. Charlottesville: University of Virginia Press, 1983.

_______. James I., Jr. *Stonewall Jackson: The Man, the Soldier, the Legend*. New York: MacMillan, 1997.

Ryan, Thomas J. "Rumors of Invasion. Lee Plans While Hooker Counters, Mid May to Early June, 1863." *The Gettysburg Magazine*, Vol. 41, July, 2013, pp. 7–14.

Schildt, John W. *Hunter Holmes McGuire: Stonewall Jackson's Doctor.* Shippensburg, Pa.: White Mane Books, 2002.

_______. *Stonewall Jackson Day by Day.* Chewsville, Md.: Antietam Publications, 1980.

Starr, Stephen Z. *The Union Cavalry in the Civil War, Vol. II.* Baton Rouge: Louisiana State University Press, 1981.

Stephens, Robert G. *Intrepid Warrior: Clement Anselm Evans, Confederate General from Georgia.* Dayton, Ohio: Morningside, 1992.

Strader, Eloise C., ed. *The Civil War Journal of Mary Greenhow Lee of Winchester, Virginia.* Winchester, Va.: Winchester-Frederick County Historical Society, 2011.

Summers, Festus T. *The Baltimore and Ohio in the Civil War.* New York: G.P. Putnam's Sons, 1939.

Tanner, R. G. *Stonewall in the Valley: Thomas J. "Stonewall" Jackson's Shenandoah Valley Campaign, Spring, 1862.* New York: Doubleday & Co., 1976.

Tayloe, Monty."Valley's bloodiest battlefield preserved for $3.35 million." *Winchester Star,* November 11, 2008.

Tischler, Allan. "Forgotten in the Valley." *Civil War News.* February–March, 2013.

Tischler, Allan Collection, 208 WFCHS/THL, Stewart Bell Jr. Archives, Handley Regional Library, Winchester, VA, USA.

Tucker, Spencer C. *Brigadier General John D. Imboden: Confederate Commander in the Shenandoah.* Lexington, Ky.: The University Press of Kentucky, 2003.

Vandiver, Frank E. *Jubal's Raid: General Early's Famous Attack on Washington in 1864.* New York: McGraw Hill Book Co., 1960.

_______. *Mighty Stonewall.* New York: New York: McGraw Hill Book Co., 1937.

Walsh, Jack. *Military Histories of Confederate Generals.* Kent, Ohio: Kent State University Press, 1995.

Warner, Ezra J. *Generals in Blue: Lives of the Union Commanders.* Baton Rouge: Louisiana State University Press, 1964.

_______. *Generals in Gray: Lives of the Confederate Commanders.* Baton Rouge: Louisiana State University Press, 1959.

Wells, Dean M. "Ewell Seizes the Day at Winchester." *America's Civil War* (March 1997): 46–54.

Wert, Jeffry D. *Custer.* New York: Simon & Shuster, 1996.

_______. *From Winchester to Cedar Creek.* Carlisle, Pa.: South Mountain Press, 1987.

Wheeler, Richard. *Sword over Richmond: An Eye-Witness History of McClellan's Peninsula Campaign.* New York: Harper & Row, 1986.

_______. *Witness to Gettysburg.* New York: Harper & Row, 1987.

Williams, T. Harry. *Hayes of the Twenty-Third: The Civil War Volunteer Officer.* New York: A. A. Knopf, 1965.

Wise, Jennings. *The Long Arm of Lee.* New York: Oxford University Press, 1959.